READ IT AGAIN!

▬ More Book 2 ▬
A Guide for Teaching Reading Through Literature

Liz Rothlein, Ed.D
Terri Christman, M.Ed.

Illustrated by Toni Summers

GoodYearBooks
An Imprint of ScottForesman
A Division of HarperCollinsPublishers

Good Year Books

are available for preschool through grade 6 for every basic curriculum subject plus many enrichment areas. For more Good Year Books, contact your local bookseller or educational dealer. For a complete catalog with information about other Good Year Books, please write:

Good Year Books
Scott, Foresman and Company
1900 East Lake Avenue
Glenview, Illinois 60025

ISBN 0-673-36007-5

1 2 3 4 5 6 MAL 95 94 93 92 91 90

CONTENTS

INTRODUCTION

Rationale

Current literature reveals that using trade books to teach reading is gaining in popularity. For example, Bernice E. Cullinan (1987), former International Reading Association president, has written and spoken about the power of trade books to overcome "aliteracy," a term used for those who can read but don't or won't read. William Bennett (1986), former U.S. Secretary of Education, has recommended using more trade books in the elementary classroom as a way to overcome "the dreadening quality of what children are given to read." Bill Honig, State Superintendent of Public Education, implemented the California Reading Initiative Program, which consists of curriculum guidebooks to accompany over a thousand trade books recommended for the classroom.

One motivation for integrating trade books into the curriculum is research showing convincingly that reading to and with children works best in fostering literacy (Doake, 1979; Durkin, 1966; Holdaway, 1979; International Reading Association, 1986a, 1986b; Schickedanz, 1983, 1986). Recognizing the importance of childhood reading experiences, First Lady Barbara Bush recently announced the formation of the Barbara Bush Foundation for Family Literacy, which will give grants to programs that focus on the family as the key to a more literate nation. In addition to learning to read, children develop personal preferences and special interests in books through this early exposure to literature and are thereby motivated to pursue books of their own choice. Proponents of literature-based reading programs agree that their success should be measured in terms of the number of students who eventually establish the habit of reading for independent learning, personal pleasure, and continued growth.

The attitudes children develop toward reading are also of great importance. As Bruno Bettelheim (1981) so poignantly stated, "A child's attitude toward reading is of such importance that, more often than not, it determines his scholastic fate. Moreover, his experience in learning to read may decide how he will feel about learning in general, and even about himself as a person." Ulrich Hardt (1983) has supported this view: "Children will become readers only if their emotions have been engaged, their imaginations stirred and stretched by what they find on printed pages. One sure way to make this happen is through literature."

Integrating literature into the curriculum does not mean abandoning the basal reader. Trade books can be used to supplement and enhance the basal reader program. Cullinan (1987) has reported that, even though 85 to 90 percent of the elementary classrooms in the United States use the basal reading series as the core instructional material, no basal series was ever intended to be a complete, self-contained reading program. Therefore, teachers must learn techniques for integrating literature into the curriculum and acquire materials for doing so.

Many publishers are responding by publishing guidebooks, kits, and the like to aid teachers. *Read It Again! More Book 2*, the fourth in a series of guidebooks written by Liz Rothlein and Terri Christman, provides instructors with imaginative teaching ideas to complement fifteen easily accessible, popular, quality children's books. Students in grades three through five will benefit from activities emphasizing the interactive processes of speaking, listening, reading, and writing. These activities involve the children in music, art, process writing, cooking, geography, and poetry. The discussion questions suggested for each book reflect the taxonomy developed by B. S. Bloom and others (1956) and focus on higher-order thinking skills, requiring students to analyze, synthesize, and evaluate.

Read It Again! More Book 2 can be adapted to almost any classroom setting. It will be particularly beneficial to resource room teachers, teachers in gifted programs, and librarians. The activities can be presented to large or small groups, are designed for different levels of ability, and can be used to encourage independent work.

Read It Again! More Book 2 is also an excellent resource for parents. The suggested books and activities will help parents develop their children's appreciation for literature and reading, as well as the skills necessary to become effective and involved readers.

Objectives

Read It Again! More Book 2 is designed to enable students to develop vital thinking and learning skills. The activities will help students meet the following objectives, developed by the National Council of Teachers of English (1983):

- Realize the importance of literature as a mirror of human experience, reflecting human motives, conflicts, and values
- Be able to identify with fictional characters in human situations as a means of relating to others; gain insights from involvement with literature
- Become aware of important writers representing diverse backgrounds and traditions in literature
- Become familiar with masterpieces of literature, both past and present
- Develop effective ways of talking and writing about varied forms of literature
- Experience literature as a way to appreciate the rhythms and beauty of the language
- Develop habits of reading that carry over into adult life

Features

Read It Again! More Book 2 focuses on the following fifteen easy-to-find books, listed by suggested reading level. These books have a proven track record of success with children. Several of them are Newbery Award winners.

Third-Grade Reading Level
Be a Perfect Person in Just Three Days by Stephen Manes
Bunnicula by Deborah and James Howe
The Courage of Sarah Noble by Alice Dalgliesh
Freckle Juice by Judy Blume
The Velveteen Rabbit by Margery Williams

Fourth-Grade Reading Level
Dear Mr. Henshaw by Beverly Cleary
How to Eat Fried Worms by Thomas Rockwell
Pippi Longstocking by Astrid Lindgren
Rent a Third Grader by B. B. Hiller
Stuart Little by E. B. White

Fifth-Grade Reading Level

The Borrowers by Mary Norton
Fantastic Mr. Fox by Roald Dahl
Island of the Blue Dolphins by Scott O'Dell
Tuck Everlasting by Natalie Babbitt
A Wrinkle in Time by Madeleine L'Engle

Note: The books are listed by reading level; the interest level of the books spans grades three through seven.

The following basic information is provided for each book: author, illustrator, publisher and publication date, number of pages, reading and interest levels, other works by the same author, and information about the author.

Next comes a summary of the book and an introduction to use when presenting the book to children. Key vocabulary words from the story are then listed. Next are discussion questions designed to foster higher-level thinking skills and bulletin board ideas offered as reinforcement activities. Many of these activities require whole-class participation with minimal teacher direction.

The major feature of the book is the reproducible activity sheets provided for each selection. These activity sheets can easily be correlated with basic objectives in language arts, literature, and the social sciences. For flexibility and ease of use, the activity sheets have been numbered according to level of difficulty, Activity Sheet 1 being the easiest, and Activity Sheet 3 the most difficult. However, all three activity sheets may be used by one student: Activity Sheet 1 could be considered an independent activity, Activity Sheet 2 an instructional activity, and Activity Sheet 3 an enrichment activity. Teachers and parents can determine which activities are most appropriate for each child's individual needs.

Finally, in addition to the reproducible activity sheets, optional ideas for activities are also provided. These include activities for group and individual participation.

The Appendix contains general activity sheets that can be used after all the selected books in *Read It Again! More Book 2* have been read. These activity sheets can be reproduced or can be fastened to tagboard and laminated, then used in an independent learning center. Also in the Appendix is a selection of book report forms and a list of all the vocabulary words introduced for the selected books. This list of words can be used to create additional reinforcement activities. Finally, an answer key to activities is provided for teachers' and parents' convenience.

Guidelines for Developing Book Units

Teachers may find that some of their students' favorite books are not available in guidebooks like *Read It Again!* series. By following some simple guidelines, teachers can develop their own "book units" based on books of their choice:

1. Select the book, taking the following into consideration:
   a. Use books that are well written. Children especially enjoy stories with a strong, fast-paced plot and memorable, interesting, well-delineated characters they can identify with.
   b. Select books that reflect students' interests. Use interest inventories and talk with your students about what they like. Books are more appealing when they relate to specific interests or when students can identify with the characters, learning how others deal with situations

and problems similar to their own experiences.
   c. Select books that will stimulate their imaginations.
   d. Select books from a variety of genres. Books of fiction (realistic fiction, historical fiction, fantasy, folklore) provide students with characters and emotions they can identify with, establish settings and themes that captivate their imaginations, and explore the human condition. Poetry should be included, too. Nonfiction books (informational books and biographies) arm students with the facts and background they'll need to connect new concepts and knowledge.
   e. Select books that represent both traditional and modern literature. Modern literature reflects contemporary settings, themes, language, and characters. Traditional literature provides links with the past and carries readers to another place and time.
   f. Select several books by the same author to help students gain an appreciation for the style and works of authors of outstanding children's literature.
   g. Select books that cover a specific theme or concept currently being developed in class.

2. Once the book has been selected, develop the unit using the following information:
   a. Title of book
   b. Names of author and illustrator
   c. Publisher and date of publication
   d. Number of pages
   e. Reading level
   f. Interest level
   g. Other books by the author
   h. Information about the author: This information can be found in *Something About the Author: Facts and Pictures About Authors and Illustrators of Books for Young Children* and *Yesterday's Authors for Children.*
   i. Summary of the book: The summary helps you remember what the book is about; it also helps students decide if they want to read the book. The summary should identify the main characters and, in a short statement, reveal the plot.
   j. Introduction to the book: The introduction needs to provide a purpose or motivation for reading the book. The introduction often includes a statement that relates to readers or asks a question that can be answered once the book has been read.
   k. Key vocabulary words: Select and define some of the words that students may not be familiar with and that are important to understanding the story.
   l. Discussion questions: Asking good questions is one of the most vital aspects of developing comprehension and thinking skills. After asking a question, give students time to reflect on possible responses. A wait of 3 to 5 seconds is generally recommended. Often you will have to rephrase a question, depending on students' level of understanding. Good questions:
     • Are relevant and meaningful: Asking too many questions interferes with students' enjoyment of the story. Questions that are unrelated to the story's theme or that simply require students to answer with facts

stated in the book do little to enhance comprehension and higher-order thinking.

• Foster higher-level thinking: Although literal questions (testing knowledge and comprehension) are important to ascertain students' understanding of the story, questions should be included that ask students to analyze ("what is the reason that," "what are the causes," "what are the consequences," "examine evidence"), synthesize ("create," "devise," "design"), and evaluate ("what is good/bad," "what do you like best," "judge the evidence"). These higher-order questions are especially important for fostering critical and creative thinking.

• Help students reach an understanding of an issue or concept: Questions should flow and reflect a sense of continuity, rather than being isolated, so students will be guided to form their own conclusions and judgments.

• Encourage application of background knowledge, ideas, and experiences. Questions should help students bring out what they have already experienced or learned and then integrate it with information found in the book.

   m. Bulletin board: Create a bulletin board that relates to the book, and give students a chance to participate in constructing it.

   n. Activity sheets: Construct activity sheets that relate to some aspect of the book as well as the competencies being taught in the curriculum. For example, if students are working on letter writing, after reading *Charlotte's Web* they can write a letter to Mr. Arable telling him why he should not kill Wilbur.

   o. Additional activities: Create an ongoing list of activities that relate to the book. These may include art, drama, movement, cooking, science, and social studies activities.

3. Develop an organizational system for storing and filing the book units, such as file folders, small boxes, or manila envelopes. The book, bulletin board letters, and other related materials can then be kept together from year to year. Eventually, you will have a collection of book units.

Guidelines for Using This Book

Before using the activities in *Read It Again! More Book 2*, you should present each of the selected books in an interesting and meaningful way. Students should enjoy themselves, as well as develop skills that will benefit them as they read on their own. One way of presenting the books to students is through reading aloud. The following suggestions may be helpful:

• Establish a regular schedule for reading aloud.
• Practice reading the book to acquaint yourself with the story's concepts in advance.
• Have a prereading session to set the stage. Include the title of the book, the author's and illustrator's names, an introduction or purpose for listening to the story, an introduction of key vocabulary words, and a discussion about the main parts of the book, such as the book jacket, end pages, author information, and so on.
• Create a comfortable atmosphere in which distractions are minimal.
• Read with feeling and expression. Pay careful attention to vocal pitch and stress so spoken dialogue sounds like conversation.
• When appropriate, hold the book so everyone can see the print and the illustrations.

- Allow the children to participate in the story when appropriate. Occasionally, you may want to stop and ask students what they think might happen next or how the story may end.
- Provide opportunities to respond to the story. Although it is not necessary for students to respond to every story, they can benefit from such follow-up activities as discussion questions, dramatizations, art activities, book reports, and so on.

Another way of presenting books to students is through a silent reading period, often referred to as sustained silent reading (SSR). SSR provides students with an opportunity to read independently. The following suggestions may be helpful in setting up an SSR program in your classroom:

- Provide students with a wide selection of books to choose from.
- Allow time for students to browse through the books and select one to read.
- Provide a regular time each day for SSR so students come to expect this period as a permanent part of their routine.
- Start the program with 5 to 10 minutes of reading, depending on students' abilities, then gradually increase the time.
- Make sure everyone reads, including the teacher.
- Allow a time at the end of SSR for students to share what they have read. Ask such questions as "What is something interesting you read about today?" "What characters did you like best?" "Why?"

The flexible format of *Read It Again! More Book 2* allows you to use it in a variety of ways. The books and many of the activities can be presented in any order, although the following format is suggested:

1. Introduce the selected book.
2. Introduce the vocabulary words.
3. Read the book aloud, or provide individual copies of the book and time for students to read it themselves.
4. Ask the discussion questions.
5. Put up the bulletin board.
6. Introduce the activity sheet(s).
7. Do appropriate additional activities.
8. Provide appropriate general activities.

The amount of time allotted to each book will depend on several factors, including age and grade level of the students and flexibility of time and scheduling.

Whatever you do, have fun and get students addicted to books!

References

Bennett, William J. *First Lessons: A Report on Elementary Education in America*. Washington, D.C.: U.S. Government Printing Office, 1986.

Bettelheim, Bruno. "Attitudes Toward Reading." *Atlantic Monthly*, Nov. 1981, p. 25.

Bloom, B. S., M. B. Englehart, S. J. Furst, W. H. Hill, and D. R. Krathwohl. *Taxonomy of Educational Objectives. The Classification of Educational Goals. Handbook I: Cognitive Domain*. New York: Longmans Green, 1956.

Cullinan, Bernice E. (ed.). *Children's Literature in the Reading Program*. Newark, Del.: International Reading Association, 1987.

Doake, David. "Book Experience and Emergent Reading Behavior." Paper presented at preconvention institute no. 24, Research on Written

Language Development, International Reading Association annual convention, Atlanta, Georgia, April 1979.

Durkin, Dolores. *Children Who Read Early*. New York: Teachers' College Press, 1966.

Hardt, Ulrich. *Teaching Reading with the Other Language Arts*. Newark, Del.: International Reading Association, 1983, p. 108.

Holdaway, Don. *The Foundations of Literacy*. Toronto: Ashton Scholastic, 1979.

International Reading Association. "IRA Position Statement on Reading and Writing in Early Childhood." *The Reading Teacher*, Oct. 1986a, vol. 39, pp. 822–824.

International Reading Association. "Literacy Development and Pre-First Grade: A Joint Statement of Concerns About Present Practices in Pre-First Grade Reading Instruction and Recommendation for Improvement." *Young Children*, Nov. 1986b, vol. 41, pp. 10–13.

National Council of Teachers of English. "Essentials of English." *Language Arts*, Feb. 1983, vol. 60, pp. 244–248.

Schickedanz, J. *Helping Children Learn About Reading*. Washington, D.C.: National Association for the Education of Young Children, 1983.

Schickedanz, J. *More Than the ABCs: The Early Stages of Reading and Writing*. Washington, D.C.: National Association for the Education of Young Children, 1986.

SELECTED BOOKS AND ACTIVITIES

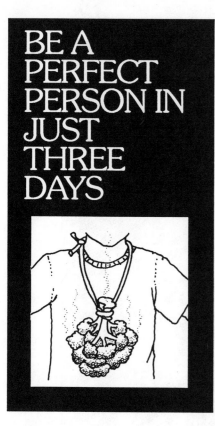

BE A PERFECT PERSON IN JUST THREE DAYS

Author
Stephen Manes

Illustrator
Tom Huffman

Publisher
Clarion Books, 1982

Pages 76	Reading Level Gr. 3	Interest Level Gr. 3–7

Other Books by the Manes
The Hooples' Haunted House; The Boy Who Turned into a TV Set; Slim Down Camp; Socko: Every Riddle Your Feet Will Ever Find; Clash of the Titan's Storybook; That Game from Outer Space; First Strange Thing That Happened to Oscar Noodleman

Information About the Author

Stephen Manes was born on January 8, 1949 in Pittsburgh, Pennsylvania. He has written over a dozen books for children and young adults plus several screenplays. He displays a humorous and nonsensical writing style in his children's books. He reveals a more serious side as a writer of young adult novels.

Stephen Manes has been writing books for as long as he can remember. His appetite was whetted when he was in the third grade and he became a roving reporter for the school newspaper, the *Sunnyside Review*. He was promoted to feature editor, news editor, and then editor in chief. He also won several statewide prizes for comic poems.

He believes that writing books for children allows him to cultivate a sense of silliness and whimsy that, unfortunately, many adults seem to lack.

Summary

Be a Perfect Person in Just Three Days is a humorous story about a boy named Milo, who happens upon a do-it-yourself book on how to become perfect in three days. Milo follows the instructions of the book's author, Dr. K. Pinkerton Silverfish, and finds himself doing some rather odd things, such as wearing broccoli around his neck, not eating for 24 hours, and doing nothing for 24 hours. In the end, Milo finds out that being perfect is not all he thought it would be. Instead, it is boring and not much fun.

Introduction

Dr. Silverfish, the author of *Be a Perfect Person in Just Three Days*, has written a book that tells how to become perfect. Milo, taking the book's advice, must wear broccoli around his neck for one day, not eat for 24 hours, and do nothing (including sleeping) for 24 hours. Do you think if you read a book telling you to do these things that you would do them? Why or why not?

Vocabulary Words

perfection	precisely	smirking	outsmarted
essential	glowered	scanned	humiliating
astonishment	consumption		

From *Read It Again! More Book 2* published by GoodYearBooks. Copyright © 1991 Liz Rothlein and Terri Christman.

BE A PERFECT PERSON IN JUST THREE DAYS

From *Read It Again! More Book 2* published by GoodYearBooks. Copyright © 1991 Liz Rothlein and Terri Christman.

Discussion Questions

1 Do you think Dr. K. Pinkerton Silverfish is a good author? Why or why not? (answers may vary)

2 Why did Milo decide to read the book *Be a Perfect Person in Just Three Days*? (answers may vary but might include because the book fell off the shelf and hit him on the head, because it was a thin book and wouldn't take long to read, or because Milo wanted to be perfect)

3 What were some of the things Milo did that made him feel he wasn't perfect? (answers may vary but might include getting into dumb accidents like knocking over his mother's expensive bud vase, sitting on his sister's new record album, or letting the bottom fall out of a bag of groceries)

4 When Milo's family asked him why he was wearing broccoli around his neck, what did he say? (they were studying nutrition at school and he was one of the vegetables)

5 What was Dr. Silverfish's reason for having Milo wear the broccoli around his neck? (answers may vary but might include so Milo could prove he had courage)

6 Why do you think Milo didn't explain his strange behavior by telling his family and friends about the book, *Be a Perfect Person in Just Three Days*? (he thought everyone would laugh at him)

7 What was Dr. Silverfish's purpose for not allowing Milo to eat for 24 hours? (answers may vary but might include so Milo could prove he had willpower)

8 How do you feel about Mr. Crinkley, Milo's father? (answers may vary)

9 What is the most important thing that Milo learned from reading *Be a Perfect Person in Just Three Days*? (answers may vary)

Bulletin Board

In bold letters, put the caption "THE MOST PERFECT THING ABOUT ME IS . . . " on the bulletin board. Then ask each student to complete that sentence, put his or her name on the paper, and fasten it to the bulletin board.

Name _____ Date _____

**ACTIVITY
SHEET 1**

Directions
Dr. Silverfish told Milo to watch for his new book, *Make Four Billion Dollars by Next Thursday!* Pretend you are Dr. Silverfish's publisher. In the space provided, create a full-page ad for this book.

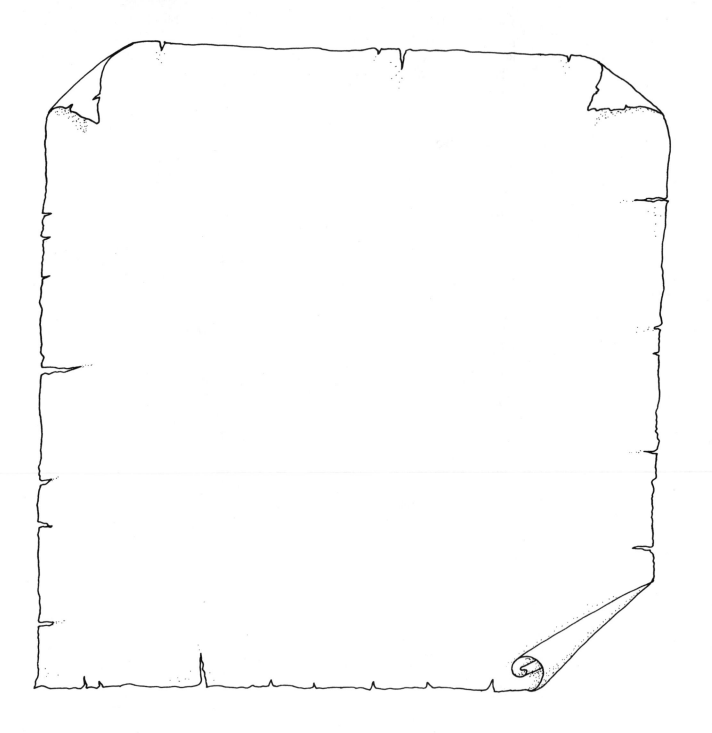

BE A PERFECT PERSON IN JUST THREE DAYS

ACTIVITY SHEET 2

Directions
The following words are found in the book, *Be a Perfect Person in Just Three Days*. Match the words with their meanings, and then write a sentence using each word.

a. having no use
b. full of juice, juicy
c. card game played by one person
d. to take more time than is necessary
e. having a strong smell or taste
f. to float through the air or over water

g. to invent, recite, or compare without preparation
h. stupid person
i. to merely exist
j. sarcastic

1. _____ pungent _____

_____

2. _____ waft _____

_____

3. _____ moron _____

_____

4. _____ snide _____

_____

5. _____ vegetate _____

_____

6. _____ succulent _____

_____

7. _____ dawdle _____

_____

8. _____ futile _____

_____

9. _____ improvise _____

_____

10. _____ solitaire _____

_____

Name _____ Date _____

Directions
List ten things you think you could do to become a perfect person:

1. _____

2. _____

3. _____

4. _____

5. _____

6. _____

7. _____

8. _____

9. _____

10. _____

Would you like to be a perfect person? _____ Why or why not? _____

_____

_____

Who is the most perfect person you know? _____

What does this person do to make him or her perfect? _____

_____

_____

BE A PERFECT PERSON IN JUST THREE DAYS

Additional Activities

1 Ask students to write a recipe for becoming perfect. Be creative! For example:

> **Perfection**
>
> 1½ cups of self-confidence
> ½ cup of willpower
> ¼ cup of courage
> 1 teaspoon of kindness
> ½ teaspoon of humbleness
> pinch of sensitivity
>
> Mix the ingredients together and you have perfection!

2 Pair students. Tell one student of each pair to list five things about the other that he or she thinks are perfect, whether they relate to physical appearance, actions, or whatever. Have students switch places and then share their lists.

3 *Be a Perfect Person in Just Three Days* by Dr. K. Pinkerton Silverfish is a very short book. As a writing activity, ask students to create their own stories about how to become perfect in just three days. Combine these stories into a class book for everyone to read.

4 Dr. Silverfish said he had to be going because one of his Venus flytraps was attacking his most unusual toothpick. A Venus flytrap, an insectivorous plant that lives in the southeastern United States, closes and traps insects. Ask students to research the Venus flytrap. Finally, allow time to share the findings.

5 *Bartlett's Book of Familiar Quotations* contains many quotations on a variety of subjects. Tell students to find quotations on perfection and to write the one they like best on a piece of paper. Then ask them to write their own quotation about perfection. Finally, provide time to share these quotations.

BUNNICULA

Authors
Deborah and James Howe

Illustrator
Alan Daniel

Publisher
Avon Books, 1979

Pages	Reading Level	Interest Level
98	Gr. 3	Gr. 3–5

Other Books by the Howes
Teddy Bear's Scrapbook

Information About the Authors

James and Deborah Howe were husband and wife. They wrote two books together before she died of cancer in 1978. It was Deborah who suggested that they collaborate on a children's book based on a character (Count Bunnicula) James had created several years earlier in an uncontrolled fit of whimsy. This project started a whole new career for them as authors of children's books.

James Howe has remarried and lives in Manhattan. He continues to write because he finds writing rewarding and fulfilling.

Summary

The Monroe family find a bunny at the movie theater. They are watching a Dracula movie so they name the bunny Bunnicula. When they bring him home, Harold the dog thinks the bunny is a new pet. But Chester the cat thinks Bunnicula is a vampire bunny. Bunnicula's markings make him look like he is wearing a cape, and he seems to have fangs. Strange things seem to happen around the house after Bunnicula arrives. So Chester, with a little help from Harold, tries to rescue the family from the vampire bunny.

Introduction

Look at the cover of the book. Describe what you see. What do you think this story is about?

Vocabulary Words

admonition	subtle	fraught	digress
indulgent	trundled	reverie	alert
overwrought	tranquil	exhausted	rivalry
repulsive	stealthily	narrative	

BUNNICULA

Discussion Questions

1 Who is telling the story? (Harold)

2 Why did the family decide to name the bunny Bunnicula? (they found him at a Dracula movie)

3 Why did Chester think Bunnicula was a vampire? (answers may vary but might include because Bunnicula had markings on his back that made it look as if he was wearing a cape, because he seemed to have two fangs, because he slept during the day, or because he could get out of his locked cage)

4 Which character did you like best? Explain. (answers may vary)

5 Do you have a pet? If so, tell us what kind of pet you have, its name, and something funny or unusual it has done. If you do not have a pet, tell us what pet you would like to have and the name you would give it. (answers may vary)

6 How did Chester try to warn the family about Bunnicula being a vampire? (Chester draped a towel around him to look like a cape, his eyes were wide and staring, his teeth were showing, he bit Harold on the neck, and so on)

7 What do you think happened to the vegetables? (answers may vary)

8 What was special about Chester? Harold? Bunnicula? (answers may vary)

Bulletin Board

Label the bulletin board "MY UNUSUAL PET." Give each student a sheet of drawing paper that measures $8\frac{1}{2} \times 11$ inches. Have them draw a picture, bring in a picture, or cut a picture from a magazine of a pet they have, have had, or would like to have. Underneath each picture, they should write the pet's name, a description of its appearance, and a description of something unusual it has done or may do.

BUNNICULA Name _____ Date _____

Directions
Read each sentence below and think about the character it best describes. Then write the sentence next to the correct character. Also, create an illustration of each character in the boxes provided.

1. He was sitting in a shoebox with a piece of paper tied with a ribbon around his neck.
2. He was telling this story.
3. He developed a taste for reading early in life.
4. He got to eat the steak.
5. He drank carrot juice.
6. He tried to warn the family about the vampire bunny.

Harold

Bunnicula

Chester

From *Read It Again! More Book 2* published by GoodYearBooks. Copyright © 1991 Liz Rothlein and Terri Christman.

BUNNICULA | Name _____ Date _____

Directions
Some things in *Bunnicula* could happen in real life (reality).
Some things could not happen in real life (fantasy). Read the
sentences below. Circle the correct word for each sentence.

reality   fantasy   1. The Monroes went to see a Dracula movie.

reality   fantasy   2. Chester read *Jonathon Livingston Seagull*.

reality   fantasy   3. Chester chased Bunnicula.

reality   fantasy   4. Harold wrote the story *Bunnicula*.

reality   fantasy   5. Harold and Chester spoke to each other.

reality   fantasy   6. Toby fed Harold chocolate cupcakes with cream filling.

reality   fantasy   7. Chester bit Harold on the neck.

reality   fantasy   8. Bunnicula slept all day.

reality   fantasy   9. Bunnicula got out of his cage without breaking anything or
opening any doors.

reality   fantasy   10. Mrs. Monroe took Chester, Harold, and Bunnicula to see the
veterinarian.

Now create two of your own reality sentences and two of your own fantasy
sentences.

Reality

1. _____

_____

2. _____

_____

Fantasy

1. _____

_____

2. _____

_____

BUNNICULA   Name _____ Date _____

Directions

Complete the following:

1. The Monroes brought home from the movie theater a small black and white rabbit. They could not decide what to name it.

How did they solve the problem? _____

_____

How would you solve the problem? _____

_____

2. Mrs. Monroe wanted to take her coat off, but she was holding the bunny. Both Toby and Pete wanted to hold the bunny. They argued about it.

How did Mrs. Monroe solve the problem? _____

_____

How would you solve the problem? _____

_____

3. The vegetables all turned white.

How did the Monroes solve the problem? _____

_____

How would you solve the problem? _____

_____

4. Identify another problem in the story.

How was it solved in the story? _____

_____

How would you solve the problem? _____

_____

5. Identify a problem you have had at some time in your life. _____

_____

How did you solve it? _____

From *Read It Again! More Book 2* published by GoodYearBooks. Copyright © 1991 Liz Rothlein and Terri Christman.

BUNNICULA

Additional Activities

1   Discuss with students the fact that Bunnicula was found at a Dracula movie and that was where his name came from. Have students get together in small groups and create a list of movie titles. Next have them list a type of animal for each movie title and create a name for that animal. Allow them time to share the names of the animals with the entire class. You may want to have students choose one of the animals and create an illustration of it, along with the movie that inspired its name.

2   The main characters of this story are Bunnicula the bunny, Chester the cat, and Harold the dog. Invite someone from a pet store to come in with these types of animals or other animals. Ask them to discuss their habits, care, expense, and so on. Students might want to create questions before the pet store representative comes. Afterward, they could write thank you notes to the guest who came to speak.

3   Let the class discuss whether they believe Bunnicula was a vampire bunny. Start by listing the reasons/evidence indicating he was a vampire bunny on one side of the chalkboard. On the other side, list the reasons/ evidence indicating he was not a vampire. Let students refer to the book as much as possible and express their own thoughts. Once all evidence has been presented, ask students to take a position and create a paragraph backing it with the information collected from the group.

4   Many different vegetables were mentioned in this story, including beans, peas, squash, tomatoes, lettuce, zucchini, and carrots. Select one of these vegetables and discuss the many ways it can be eaten, such as cooked, raw, juiced, and baked in cakes, cookies, and muffins. Following this discussion, plan a tasting party and ask each student or group of students to bring in a dish using the chosen vegetable.

5   Many books have been written about rabbits. Provide space on a shelf or table and then encourage students to bring in books about rabbits, such as *The Velveteen Rabbit* by Margery Williams, *The Tortoise and the Hare* by Janet Stevens, *Rabbit Ears* by Alfred Slote, *Rabbit Finds a Way* by Judy Delton, *Rabbit Hill* by Robert Lawson, and *Rabbit Spring* by Tilde Michels. Allow time for students to share the books.

THE COURAGE OF SARAH NOBLE

Author
Alice Dalgliesh

Illustrator
Leonard Weisgard

Publisher
Scribner's, 1974

Pages 54	Reading Level Gr. 3	Interest Level Gr. 2–5

Other Books by Dalgliesh
Bears on Hemlock Mountain; Fourth of July Story; Little Wooden Farmer; Thanksgiving Story; The Silver Pencil

Information About the Author
Alice Dalgliesh was born on October 17, 1893 in Trinidad, British West Indies and died on June 11, 1979 in Woodbury, Connecticut. Throughout her life she was an educator, book reviewer, and author. She was an elementary school teacher for 17 years. In addition, she taught children's literature at Columbia University.

Alice Dalgliesh wrote more than forty books for children. She was the first president of the Children's Book Council. Her books *The Silver Pencil, The Courage of Sarah Noble*, and *Bears on Hemlock Mountain* were all named as Newbery Honor books.

Summary
During the early 1700s, Sarah Noble, a charming and brave eight-year-old, accompanies her father into the wilderness of Connecticut to build a home. Throughout her encounters with the dark forest and the Indians, she keeps remembering what her mother said: "Keep up your courage!" Although it is difficult at times for Sarah to do this, she does. As a result, she feels good about herself. This book is based on a true story.

Introduction
During the early 1700s, Sarah Noble, an eight-year-old girl, volunteered to accompany her father into the wilderness to build a house. Although many times she was afraid and would have preferred not to be where she was, she kept her courage. Have you ever been in a situation where you felt it took a lot of courage not to give up or turn back?

Vocabulary Words

squaw	solemn	pestle	outlandish
heather	wigwam	impatience	quivers
savages	mortar	palisade	moccasins

THE COURAGE OF SARAH NOBLE

Discussion Questions

1   Do you think it was a good idea for Sarah to accompany her father on such a trip? Why or why not? (answers may vary)

2   How did it happen that Sarah went with her father into the wilderness to build a house? (answers may vary but might include that she volunteered, that her mother couldn't go because of the baby, or that she could cook)

3   Why was Sarah's red cloak so important to Sarah? (answers may vary but might include because it was something from home and made her feel secure)

4   Where did Sarah want to build a house like the Robinsons' house? (in a cave with a shed and fence)

5   Why didn't Sarah want to build a house like the Robinsons' house? (because there was no love in the Robinsons' house)

6   How might Sarah's life have been different if she hadn't gone into the wilderness with her father? (answers may vary)

7   In your opinion, what was the most courageous thing Sarah Noble did? (answers may vary)

8   What do you think would have happened to Sarah if something had happened to her father when he left her with the Indians and went back to get the rest of the family? (answers may vary)

9   What did Sarah's father mean when he said, "To be afraid and to be brave is the best courage of all"? (answers may vary)

Bulletin Board

In the book *The Courage of Sarah Noble,* Sarah's father builds a new home for the Noble family. Provide students with 9 × 12 inch sheets of white paper. Ask them to illustrate the house and its surroundings. Put the caption "SARAH NOBLE'S HOME" on the bulletin board, and post the illustrations of her home. Discuss the similarities and differences in the illustrations.

**ACTIVITY
SHEET 1**

Name _____ Date _____

Directions
Using the letters of Sarah Noble's name, write at least one word describing Sarah that begins with each letter. This is called an acrostic. The first one is done for you.

S <u>mart</u> _____   N _____

A _____   O _____

R _____   B _____

A _____   L _____

H _____   E _____

Using the letters of your first and last name, create an acrostic describing yourself.

First Name   **Last Name**

_____   _____

_____   _____

_____   _____

_____   _____

_____   _____

_____   _____

_____   _____

From *Read It Again! More Book 2* published by GoodYearBooks. Copyright © 1991 Liz Rothlein and Terri Christman.

THE COURAGE
OF SARAH
NOBLE

**ACTIVITY
SHEET 2**

Directions
Be creative! Complete the following:

1. If you could see courage, what color would it be? _____

Explain _____

2. If you could see fear, what color would it be? _____

Explain _____

3. What type of animal best represents courage? _____

Explain _____

4. What type of animal best represents fear? _____

Explain _____

5. What would courage sound like? _____

Explain _____

6. What would fear sound like? _____

Explain _____

7. If courage were a shape, what shape would it be? _____

Explain _____

8. If fear were a shape, what shape would it be? _____

Explain _____

Turn your paper over. On the top half of the page, illustrate what courage would look like; on the bottom half of the page, illustrate what fear would look like.

THE COURAGE OF SARAH NOBLE

ACTIVITY SHEET 3

Name _____ Date _____

Directions

Look up the word "courage" in the dictionary and write the definition:

_____

_____

_____

The title of the book suggests that Sarah Noble was courageous. Think about the story and what courage means to you. Then, on the balance scale below, list the examples of courage on one side and the examples of fear on the other.

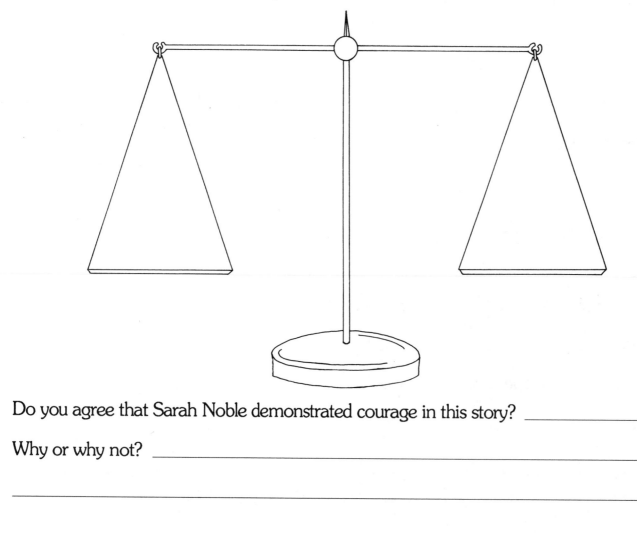

Do you agree that Sarah Noble demonstrated courage in this story? _____

Why or why not? _____

_____

_____

From *Read It Again! More Book 2* published by GoodYearBooks. Copyright © 1991 Liz Rothlein and Terri Christman.

Following the guidelines for writing a diamonte poem, create one about your own feelings of courage. A diamonte poem is written in the shape of a diamond.

Line 1: one word (a noun or a pronoun)
Line 2: two words (adjectives describing line 1)
Line 3: three words ("ing" verbs showing action related to line 1)
Line 4: four words (nouns, the first two relating to line 1, the last two to line 7)
Line 5: three words ("ing" verbs showing action, related to line 7)
Line 6: two words (adjectives describing line 7)
Line 7: one word (a noun or a pronoun, often the opposite of the word in line 1)

Additional Activities

1 *The Courage of Sarah Noble* is divided into eleven chapters. Obtain an inexpensive copy of this book or photocopy the book you have. Divide the class into eleven groups, and give each group a chapter. Ask each group to read its chapter and then, on an 18 × 24 inch sheet of paper, illustrate what happened in that chapter. After each group has completed this assignment, seat the class in a circle, beginning with the Chapter 1 group and proceeding clockwise. Next, ask each group to report in order on the chapter it was assigned and then to post the illustration representing that chapter on the wall or chalkboard. Continue until the entire story has been told and all the illustrations have been displayed.

2 Sarah Noble went with her father into the wilderness of Connecticut to cook for him. One of the many things she cooked was cornbread made from the corn her father got from the Indians. Before she could make the cornbread, the corn had to be ground using a small mortar and pestle. Obtain a mortar and pestle and some corn. Allow time for students to grind corn until it becomes cornmeal. Purchase a box of cornmeal at the market to compare with the cornmeal that the students grind. Using the following recipe, make some cornbread. Serve warm with butter.

Cornbread

1 cup of all-purpose flour
¾ cup of cornmeal
1 tablespoon of baking powder
2 tablespoons of sugar
¾ teaspoon of salt
1 egg
⅔ cup of milk
6 tablespoons of melted margarine or salad oil

Mix the first five ingredients together. In another bowl, beat the egg, milk, and margarine or oil until well blended. Stir the egg mixture into the flour mixture just until the flour is moistened (batter will be lumpy). Spread into a greased 8 × 8 inch baking pan and bake 25 minutes at 425 degrees.

---

3 Read the author's note in the front of the book, which reveals that this is a true story. Find on a map both Westfield, Massachusetts (where Sarah and her father came from) and New Milford, Connecticut (where they built their new home). Trace the most probable route they would have traveled from one place to the other. Compare what John Noble and Sarah would have seen on their trip in 1707 with what they would see on a trip between these two towns today. As a class, write a modern-day (present) version of *The Courage of Sarah Noble*.

From *Read It Again! More Book 2* published by GoodYearBooks. Copyright © 1991 Liz Rothlein and Terri Christman.

4 In addition to *The Courage of Sarah Noble*, provide students with a selection of books relating to courage such as, *Call It Courage* by Armstrong Sperry, *Island of the Blue Dolphins* by Scott O'Dell, and *Julie of the Wolves* by Jean Craighead George. After students have read the books, ask each one to nominate a character for an Academy Award for Excellence in the Field of Courage. Each student should have an opportunity to "introduce" his or her nominee, giving a brief description of the character and telling why this nominee should win the award. Finally, the class should vote on the winner of this award.

5 Tell students to write down the first thought that comes to mind in response to the following:

Courage smells like _____.

Courage tastes like _____.

Courage looks like _____.

Courage feels like _____.

Courage sounds like _____.

Allow only 30 seconds for students to write down each response. Provide time to share the answers.

FRECKLE JUICE

Author
Judy Blume

Illustrator
Sonia O. Lisker

Publisher
Dell, 1971

Pages	Reading Level	Interest Level
47	Gr. 3	Gr. 2–4

Other Books by Blume
Superfudge; Tales of a Fourth Grade Nothing; The One in the Middle Is the Green Kangaroo; Are You There God? It's Me Magaret; Blubber; Iggie's House; Otherwise Known as Sheila the Great; Then Again, Maybe I Won't

Information About the Author
Judy Blume was born in New Jersey. When she was young, she liked to pretend and made up stories in her head. Once she got to high school, she really began to write and worked on the school newspaper. She went on to college planning to be a teacher.

However, Judy Blume met her husband, lawyer John Blume, while in college. She had two children, Randy and Larry. When her children were old enough, she took writing classes at night. In 1969 she published *The One in the Middle Is the Green Kangaroo.* Since then she has published many books for young children, teenagers, and adults.

Summary
Andrew Marcus wants freckles just like Nicky Lane's. If Andrew had freckles, his mother would never know if his neck was dirty, so he wouldn't have to wash it. At school, Andrew decides to ask Nicky where he got his freckles. Sharon, a classmate, overhears and offers Andrew her secret freckle juice recipe for fifty cents. He takes the recipe home, mixes everything up, and drinks it. But instead of getting freckles, he gets very sick. Because Sharon fooled him, he decides to fool her.

Introduction
This story is about a boy who wants freckles so his mother won't know if his neck is dirty. If she doesn't know it's dirty, he won't have to wash it. What things does your mother ask you to do that you don't like to do?

Vocabulary Words

aimed	sensible	handsome	blur
drifted	wondering	manage	reflection
recipe	tilted	chattering	reminded
crept	formula	inspected	

FRECKLE JUICE

Discussion Questions

1 Which character did you like best? Why? (answers may vary)

2 Why didn't Andrew like paying Sharon fifty cents for the freckle juice recipe? (answers may vary but might include because fifty cents was a lot of money or because fifty cents was five whole weeks of allowance)

3 What ingredient would you like least in Sharon's secret recipe for freckle juice? What ingredient would you like most? (answers may vary)

4 Would you have tried the freckle juice? Why or why not? (answers may vary)

5 Explain how Andrew must have felt after he drank the freckle juice and saw no freckles? (answers may vary)

6 How did Miss Kelly make both boys feel good about themselves? (she told Andrew he was a handsome boy without freckles and told Nicky she'd hate to see him without freckles because they were a part of him)

7 Do you think having freckles would have solved Andrew's problems? Explain. (answers may vary)

8 If you have freckles, do you like them? If you don't have them, would you like to? (answers may vary)

Bulletin Board

Label the bulletin board "OUR FRECKLE JUICE RECIPES." Photocopy page 24. Have students write their own recipes to create freckles. Below the recipe, have them draw their face with freckles.

Freckle Juice

_____ (student's name)

Secret Recipe for Freckle Juice

Ingredients:

_____

_____

_____

_____

_____

Directions:

_____

_____

_____

Illustration with freckles:

From _Read It Again! More Book 2_ published by GoodYearBooks. Copyright © 1991 Liz Rothlein and Terri Christman.

FRECKLE JUICE | Name _____ Date _____

Directions

Below is a list of characters from *Freckle Juice*. Check the qualities that each character has.

	kind	tricky	mean	creative	persistent	courageous	desperate	friendly	greedy
Andrew									
Nicky									
Sharon									
Miss Kelly									
Mrs. Marcus									
You									

Select one character: _____

Write his or her qualities: _____

_____

_____

_____

_____

Name _____ Date _____

ACTIVITY SHEET 2

Directions
After looking at the picture, answer the questions.

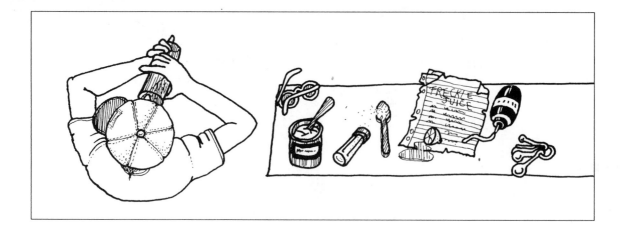

1. What is happening in this picture? _____

_____

_____

2. What happens *before* this picture in the story? _____

_____

_____

3. What happens *after* this picture in the story? _____

_____

_____

Name _____ Date _____

Directions
Read and answer the following questions.

In what ways are Andrew and Sharon alike? _____

_____

_____

_____

_____

In what ways are Andrew and Sharon different? _____

_____

_____

_____

_____

Which character is most like you, Andrew or Sharon? Explain. _____

_____

_____

_____

_____

Additional Activities

1 Have the class come up with a list of things that mothers, fathers, and caretakers make them do. List everything on the chalkboard so students can copy it. Then have students circle only the things they themselves have to do. Ask them to rank the things they do in order from what they like to do least to what they like to do most. They can share this activity in small groups or as a whole class.

2 Talk to students about Andrew Marcus wanting freckles so he wouldn't have to wash his neck each day. Discuss something they might want that someone else has and why they would want it. For example: "I would want _____'s perfect teeth so I wouldn't have to wear braces." Create a class list of things students want and why.

3 Ask students to get a picture of themselves that they can cut apart and draw on. Tell students to create a new picture of themselves by adding and deleting parts to the picture. They may want to add freckles, different hair, and so forth. For new features, they may want to use pictures in magazines or draw the ones they wish to add. Encourage students to be creative!

4 Make this recipe:

Freckle-Faced Cookies

Stir the following ingredients together in a large bowl:

1½ cups of whole wheat flour
1½ cups of graham flour
¾ teaspoon of baking powder
¾ teaspoon of salt (if desired)

Blend the remaining ingredients together in a blender:

⅔ cup of apple juice concentrate
⅔ cup of vegetable oil
1½ bananas, sliced
1½ teaspoons of cinnamon
1½ teaspoons of vanilla

Add the dry ingredients to the blended ingredients and mix thoroughly. Divide the dough in half, and roll out on a floured surface. Using a large round cookie cutter, cut out the cookies. Decorate using raisins for the eyes, nose, and mouth. Use chocolate sprinkles for freckles. Place cookies on a lightly greased cookie sheet and bake at 350 degrees for 8 minutes. Yields about thirty 3-inch cookies.

FRECKLE JUICE

5 Discuss with students how people's features and characteristics make them look different from one another. For example, some people wear glasses, some have big noses, some have freckles, some are tall. Provide students with a variety of magazines, and tell them to make a "people collage." Then have them write a poem—for example:

People
Tall people, short people,
Thin people, fat;
Lady so dainty
Wearing a hat.
Straight people, dumpy people,
Man dressed in brown,
Baby in buggy,
These make a town.
Author Unknown

THE VELVETEEN RABBIT

Author
Margery Williams

Illustrator
David Jorgensen

Publisher
Knopf, 1985

Pages 48	Reading Level Gr. 3	Interest Level Gr. 2–5

Other Books by Williams
No other books known

Information About the Author
Margery Williams was born in London, England, on July 22, 1881. At the age of nine she moved to the United States. As a child, she became very interested in nature. She walked along the Thames and through the Chelsea Pensioners' Gardens and collected caterpillars and grubs in Central Park. Her favorite book as a child was *Wood's Natural History*. Because she was the youngest child in her family, she grew up much like an only child. Instead of "people playmates," she had animals as playmates. She even raised pet mice in her dollhouse.

Margery Williams became interested in writing when she was seventeen. She interrupted her writing interests to get married, move to Paris, and have two children. She later wrote *The Velveteen Rabbit*. She died in 1944.

Summary
The Velveteen Rabbit is a magical fable of a toy rabbit who becomes a real rabbit with the help of a boy who loves and adores him.

Introduction
This is a story about a stuffed rabbit who became real. Have you ever had a stuffed animal, doll, or toy that you wished would become real?

Vocabulary Words
velveteen	sawdust	twitched	fronds
mechanical	burrows	clockwork	commonplace
shabbier	bracken	disinfected	sensitive

From *Read It Again! More Book 2* published by GoodYearBooks. Copyright © 1991 Liz Rothlein and Terri Christman.

THE VELVETEEN RABBIT

Discussion Questions

1 What did the Skin Horse mean when he said, "Real isn't how you are made, it's a thing that happens to you"? (answers may vary)

2 How did it happen that the Boy became so close to the Rabbit and slept with him every night? (Nana couldn't find the China doll at bedtime, so she gave the Boy the Rabbit)

3 What were some of the things the Rabbit enjoyed doing with the Boy? (answers may vary but might include making tunnels under the bedclothes, riding in the wheelbarrow, going on picnics, playing in fairy huts built for him, and having tea parties)

4 What were some things the Rabbit didn't enjoy about being with the boy? (answers may vary but might include being left on the lawn and getting damp, being hugged too tight, and being rolled on)

5 Did the Rabbit become real as the Skin Horse had described the idea of real? How do you know? (yes; once Nana was grumbling about the Rabbit, and the Boy sat up in bed and said, "He isn't a toy. He's REAL.")

6 How do you think the Velveteen Rabbit felt when he met the real, live rabbits out in the woods? (answers may vary)

7 How do you think the Velveteen Rabbit felt about the Fairy Flower changing him into an alive, real rabbit? (answers may vary)

8 Do you think the Rabbit recognized the Boy after he had become a real rabbit and came out of the woods to play with the other rabbits? (answers may vary)

Bulletin Board

Tell students to fasten a copy of the cinquain poems they create on Activity Sheet 3 to a sheet of paper and to draw their toys to accompany the poems. Put the caption "MY FAVORITE TOY" on the bulletin board, and then post the students' poems and illustrations.

Name _____ Date _____

Directions
Read each of the following quotes from *The Velveteen Rabbit*. In the first blank write the name of the character who said each quote. In the second blank, write the name of the character being spoken to. The characters' names are provided in the box below.

Nana	Rabbits	Fairy	Doctor	Boy	Skin Horse	Velveteen Rabbit

1. _____ to _____ "The Boy's Uncle made me be Real. That was a great many years ago; but once you are Real you can't become unreal again. It lasts for always."

2. _____ to _____ "What is Real? Does it mean having things that buzz inside you and a stick-out handle?"

3. _____ to _____ "Here, take your old Bunny! He'll go to sleep with you!"

4. _____ to _____ "Give me my Bunny! You mustn't say that. He isn't a toy. He's Real!"

5. _____ to _____ "I've brought you a new playfellow. You must be very kind to him and teach him all he needs to know in Rabbitland, for he is going to live with you forever and ever!"

6. _____ to _____ "Can you hop on your hind legs?"

7. _____ to _____ "He doesn't smell right! He isn't a rabbit at all. He isn't real!"

8. _____ to _____ "That? Why, it's a mass of scarlet fever germs! Burn it at once. What? Nonsense! Get him a new one. He mustn't have that anymore!"

9. _____ to _____ "You were Real to the Boy because he loved you. Now you shall be real to everyone."

10. _____ to _____ "Real isn't how you are made. It's a thing that happens to you."

From *Read It Again! More Book 2* published by GoodYearBooks. Copyright © 1991 Liz Rothlein and Terri Christman.

Name _____ Date _____

Directions
A fact is something that can be proven as true. For example, "Airplanes can fly" is a fact. An opinion is something that cannot be proven true. For example, "Flying is fun" is an opinion.

ACTIVITY SHEET 2

Read the following statements. Put an *F* in the blank if the statement is a fact. Put an *O* in the blank if the statement is an opinion.

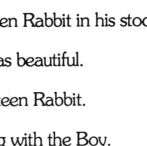

_____ 1. The Boy got the Velveteen Rabbit in his stocking as a Christmas gift.

_____ 2. The Velveteen Rabbit was beautiful.

_____ 3. The Boy liked the Velveteen Rabbit.

_____ 4. The Rabbit liked sleeping with the Boy.

_____ 5. The Rabbit was filled with sawdust.

_____ 6. The Skin Horse was real.

_____ 7. Nana didn't like the toys in the nursery.

_____ 8. The Velveteen Rabbit liked the real rabbits he saw in the woods.

_____ 9. The Boy and the Velveteen Rabbit lived in a house near the woods.

_____ 10. The real rabbits were afraid of the Velveteen Rabbit.

_____ 11. The Boy had scarlet fever.

_____ 12. All the Boy's toys had to be destroyed because of his illness.

_____ 13. A magic Fairy changed the Velveteen Rabbit into a real rabbit.

_____ 14. The Velveteen Rabbit liked being a real rabbit.

_____ 15. The boy knew his Velveteen Rabbit had become a real rabbit.

THE VELVETEEN RABBIT

**ACTIVITY
SHEET 3**

Directions

Everyone has or has had a special toy. This can be a stuffed toy like the Velveteen Rabbit or a game, a doll, a train, or something else. Think about your favorite toy and complete the following:

1. What is or was your favorite toy? _____

2. Briefly describe your toy. _____

_____

3. Do you still have your toy? _____ If yes, explain what you do with it. Do you still

play with it or use it? _____

_____

If not, what happened to your toy? _____

_____

4. When did you get your toy? _____

5. How long have you had or did you have your toy? _____

6. Who gave you the toy? _____

7. Why do you think this toy is or was your favorite? _____

_____

Write a cinquain poem about your toy. A cinquain poem is written as follows:

Line 1: one word (which may be the title)   _____

Line 2: two words (describing the title)   _____ _____

Line 3: three words (an action)   _____ _____ _____

Line 4: four words (a feeling) _____ _____ _____ _____

Line 5: one word (referring to the title)   _____

From *Read It Again! More Book 2* published by GoodYearBooks. Copyright © 1991 Liz Rothlein and Terri Christman.

THE VELVETEEN RABBIT

Additional Activities

1 Declare a "Favorite Toy Day." After students have had an opportunity to read *The Velveteen Rabbit*, set aside a specific day for them to bring in a toy that has been or perhaps still is very important to them. In preparation for "Favorite Toy Day," ask students to make a poster about their toy to display by it. This poster should include the name of the toy, why it is the student's favorite toy, special attributes of the toy, and so on.

2 Bring in a collection of books about rabbits for all ages, such as *The Little Rabbit Who Wanted Red Rings* by Carolyn Bailey, *The Tale of Peter Rabbit* by Beatrix Potter, *Mr. Rabbit and the Lovely Present* by Maurice Sendak, *The Rabbit* by John Burningham, and *Rabbit Hill* by Robert Lawson. Aileen Fischer's book of poetry, *Listen Rabbit*, may also be interesting. Encourage students to work in pairs or small groups to create a skit, puppet show, or play about rabbits that could be presented to other members of the class or to a group of kindergarten or first-grade students.

3 In the story *The Velveteen Rabbit*, all the Boy's toys, including the Velveteen Rabbit, had to be destroyed. The next night the Boy slept in a different bedroom, with a brand-new bunny. The Boy was so excited about going to the seaside the next day that he didn't care much about his new bunny or think about his old one. Discuss with students how they might have felt in a similar situation and what they think they would have done.

4 Bring in a stuffed toy to display. Ask students to write a story in which the stuffed animal becomes real. Provide time for students to illustrate the book, staple it together with a cover, and share it with the class.

5 Rabbits like carrots, and so do humans. Carrots are very healthy because they provide a good source of vitamin A. Using the word "carrot," create a webbing of all the different ways students have eaten carrots.

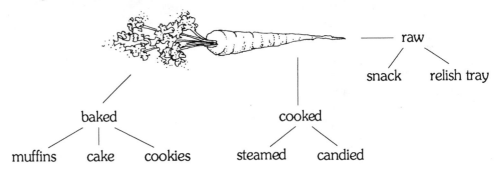

If possible, have a tasting party consisting of carrots prepared in as many ways as possible.

6 Use carrots for making prints by cutting them crosswise or lengthwise and then cutting designs on the carrots. Then dip the carrots in tempera paint and print.

DEAR MR. HENSHAW

Author
Beverly Cleary

Illustrator
Paul O'Zelinsky

Publisher
Dell, 1983

Pages 134	Reading Level Gr. 4	Interest Level Gr. 2–6

Other Books by Cleary
Ramona the Pest; Beezus and Ramona; Ellen Tebbits; Emily's Runaway Imagination; Henry Huggins; Henry and Beezus; Henry and the Clubhouse; Henry and the Paper Route; Henry and Ribsy; Mitch and Amy; The Mouse and the Motorcycle; Otis Spofford; Ramona and Her Mother; Runaway Ralph; Socks; Ramona Quimby, Age 8; Ramona Forever

Information About the Author
Beverly Cleary was born in Oregon in 1916. She lived in a thirteen-room farmhouse that was built by pioneers. She was first introduced to books by her mother, who started the first library in a nearby town. When Beverly Cleary was six years old, her family moved from the farm to the city, and her life changed drastically. She didn't like school until she was in the third grade. It was then that she first enjoyed reading.

Beverly Cleary, who became a librarian, based many of her stories on what she enjoyed as a child. Her books contain humor about real-life problems that children experience. *Dear Mr. Henshaw* won the Newbery Medal in 1984, and in 1982 *Ramona Quimby, Age 8* won the Newbery Honor Book Award. She has also received the Laura Ingalls Wilder Award.

Summary
Leigh Botts, a young boy, writes a series of letters to an author, Mr. Henshaw, and writes in his diary. Through these writings, Leigh shares his feelings about his parents' divorce and the problems he confronts at school.

Introduction
Through Leigh Botts's letter writing to his favorite author, Mr. Henshaw, and his diary writings, the reader gets a lot of insights into Leigh's development from first through sixth grade. This book shares the difficulties Leigh faces because of his parents' divorce, as well as problems he confronts at school. As you read *Dear Mr. Henshaw*, think about how Leigh dealt with his problems and other solutions you may have.

Vocabulary Words

retain	partition	fictitious	canape
nuisance	refinery	gondola	mimeographed
molest	halyard	rig	cross-country

DEAR MR. HENSHAW

Discussion Questions

1 In the beginning of the book, Leigh was signing his letters "Your number 1 fan." But by the time he answered Mr. Henshaw's third question, Leigh was signing his letter, "Your ex-friend, Leigh Botts." Why? (answers may vary)

2 What did Leigh's father mean when he said, "Well, keep your nose clean, kid"? (answers may vary)

3 What did Mr. Henshaw mean when he said he didn't have any kids because he didn't raise goats? (answers may vary)

4 Leigh loved his dog Bandit very much, but at the end of the story he gave the dog back to his dad. Do you agree with this decision? Why or why not? (answers may vary)

5 How do you think Leigh felt when he called his dad and found out there was another woman and boy in his father's life? Do you think it would have been better if Leigh had not found out about this? Why or why not? (answers may vary)

6 Leigh's father sent him a twenty-dollar bill and a paper napkin. On the napkin was written, "Sorry about Bandit. Here's $20. Go buy yourself an ice cream cone, Dad." Leigh got very angry over this. Why? (answers may vary)

7 Leigh did not seem to understand why his mother and father had gotten a divorce. Why do you think they got a divorce? (answers may vary)

8 How would you describe how Leigh felt about his father? (answers may vary)

Bulletin Board

Put a copy of Activity Sheet 1 on a large sheet of paper and fasten it to the center of the bulletin board. Put the caption "GUESS WHO I AM" on the bulletin board. Ask students to complete Activity Sheet 1 and fasten their sheets to the bulletin board. Next, provide time for students to read at least two other students' activity sheets and then, at the bottom of the sheets, sign the name of the student they think each describes along with their own name. As a culminating activity, read each of the activity sheets out loud. Find out if the guesses were correct. If not, allow three guesses from members of the class. If no one guesses who the sheet is describing, ask the person to identify himself or herself.

DEAR MR. HENSHAW

Directions

In the story *Dear Mr. Henshaw*, Mr. Henshaw asked Leigh some questions so he could get to know him better. Answer the following questions and then post your worksheet on the bulletin board. DO NOT PUT YOUR NAME ON IT. See if your classmates can guess who you are.

LEIGH BOTTS

1. What do you look like? _____

2. What is your family like? _____

3. Where do you live? _____

4. Do you have any pets? _____ Describe _____

5. What do you like to do for fun and enjoyment? _____

_____

6. What do you like best about school? _____

7. What kinds of books do you like to read? _____

_____

8. Who are your friends? _____

9. What are your hobbies? _____

10. What is your favorite TV show? _____

Draw a picture of yourself.
Who Am I?

(Guess 1) _____

Identified by _____

(Guess 2) _____

Identified by _____

From *Read It Again! More Book 2* published by GoodYearBooks. Copyright © 1991 Liz Rothlein and Terri Christman.

Name _____ Date _____

Directions

Some of Leigh's letters to Mr. Henshaw contained words that were spelled incorrectly—for example, "Keep in *tutch* (touch)." In each of the following sentences, a word is misspelled. Underline the misspelled word, and then write the word correctly on the blank provided. Use the dictionary to help you.

**ACTIVITY
SHEET 2**

_____ 1. The man is made of wax, and every time he crosses the dessert, he melts a little.

_____ 2. The boys in my class who are writing about monsters just bring in a new monster on the last page to finish off the villans with a laser.

_____ 3. He loves the feel of power when he is sitting high in his cab controling a mighty machine.

_____ 4. Truckers sometimes lose there hearing in their left ear from the wind rushing past the driver's window.

_____ 5. She used to talk a lot about her elementary school principle, who was so excited about reading that she had the whole school celebrate books and authors every April.

_____ 6. I didn't think playing penball machines in a tavern on Saturday night was fun anymore.

_____ 7. My stomache felt as if it was dropping to the floor, the way it does when I hear his voice.

_____ 8. As it turned out, Barry didn't have the right kind of battary, so we just fooled around looking at his models.

_____ 9. Well, you might say our cafeteria rang with the sound of burgler alarms.

_____ 10. I never did find out who the theif was, and now that I stop to think about it, I'm glad.

DEAR MR. HENSHAW

Name _____ Date _____

Directions

Explain in your own words what was meant by each of the following statements found in *Dear Mr. Henshaw*.

1. "Mom tried to phone him at the trailer park where, as Mom says, he hangs his hat."

_____

2. "Katy has a heart as big as stone." _____

_____

3. "Cheer up or you'll trip over your lower lip." _____

_____

4. "Your father will never grow up." _____

_____

5. "He seemed like a knight in shining armor." _____

_____

6. "I am filled with wrath." _____

_____

7. "He had to dodge the highway patrol to get home in time for Christmas." _____

_____

8. "Dad says civilization is ruining hawks." _____

_____

9. "I can't complain to the teacher because it isn't a good idea for a new boy in the

school to be a snitch." _____

From *Read It Again! More Book 2* published by GoodYearBooks. Copyright © 1991 Liz Rothlein and Terri Christman.

DEAR MR. HENSHAW

Additional Activities

1 When Leigh was in first and second grades, kids called him Leigh the Flea because he was so small. Have students create a humorous, maybe nonsensical, or even realistic name for themselves that will rhyme with their name, as "Leigh" rhymes with "flea." Provide time to share these names.

2 Leigh's father was a truck driver. Brainstorm all the reasons why truck drivers are important to our lives, and list these on the chalkboard (truckers transport fruits, vegetables, cars, animals, lumber, and so on). If possible, invite a truck driver to come into the classroom and tell students about his or her job. For additional information about trucking as a career, write to the American Trucking Association, Inc., Public Affairs, 2200 Mill Road, Alexandria, VA 22314 and ask for the brochure "Career as a Truck Driver."

3 Encourage students to select an author, as Leigh did in *Dear Mr. Henshaw*, and to write to him or her asking questions like Leigh's: "How many books have you written?" "Why do you write books for children?" "Where do you get your ideas?" Addresses for authors can be obtained from publishers of their books. In fact, most publishers will forward letters to authors.

4 Provide materials (construction paper, lined writing paper, glue, yarn, and so on) for students to make a diary. Allow students a regularly scheduled time each day (approximately 5 minutes) to write in their diaries. Remind them that diaries are personal and will not be read by anyone else.

5 Leigh's mother worked at Catering by Katy. One of the foods that his mother brought home was canapes. Divide students into four or five groups. Ask them to look through recipe books and agree on a canape recipe. Tell them to plan cooperatively and then bring in the necessary ingredients for making the recipe they've selected. Then have a canape party, arranging the classroom into "canape centers" with a recipe and the necessary ingredients grouped in one spot. Everyone can then circulate and make the different canapes.

6 Discuss Leigh's visit to the "butterfly trees," where many monarch butterflies spend the winter after flying thousands of miles. He found thousands of butterflies on one tree. Provide encyclopedias or other appropriate reference materials, and allow time for students to research the monarch butterfly. Books like *The Monarch Butterfly* by Gail Gibbons (Holiday House, 1989) may be helpful. In particular, students should find out what monarch butterflies do during the winter months. Allow time for students to share their findings.

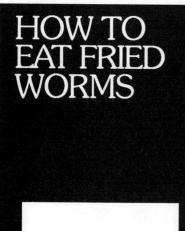

HOW TO EAT FRIED WORMS

Author
Thomas Rockwell

Illustrator
Emily McCully

Publisher
Bantam Doubleday Dell, 1973

Pages 116	Reading Level Gr. 4	Interest Level Gr. 3–6

Other Books by Rockwell
Rackety-Bang; Norman Rockwell's Hometown; Humph! Squawwwk!; The Neon Motorcycle; How to Fight a Girl

Information About the Author

Thomas Rockwell was born on March 15, 1933 in New Rochelle, New York. His father was Norman Rockwell, a famous American artist. He is married to Gail, an artist who helps illustrate some of his books. They have two children.

Thomas Rockwell started reading to his son when he was about three years old. He read from the *Oxford Book of Nursery Rhymes*, edited by Iona and Peter Opie. These nursery rhymes excited Thomas Rockwell so much that he began writing a few poems himself. From there, he went on to writing stories and picture books.

He now lives with his family on a farm that has many animals near Poughkeepsie, New York.

Summary

Billy accepts a bet that he can eat fifteen worms in fifteen days. The agreement is that Alan, the boy with whom he makes the bet, will supply the worms and that Billy can prepare them in any manner he chooses. Billy ceremoniously eats a worm each day, using such condiments as mustard, catsup, and horseradish. His family takes it all in stride. His mother even prepares one of his worms by cooking Alsatian Smothered Worms. Billy's parents also check with the family doctor. When it begins to look as if Billy will win the bet, Alan and his friend Joe try many tricks to stop him. However, the tricks are not successful, and Billy does indeed eat fifteen worms.

Introduction

Billy accepted a bet to eat fifteen worms in fifteen days. Although he could prepare the worms any way he wanted, some days he could hardly bear to eat them. Have you ever accepted a bet or a dare that you wish you hadn't accepted or that was difficult to carry through?

Vocabulary Words

obsequiously	firming	apoplectically	hauncher
menacingly	agony	chaff	jostled
clambered	gore	reassuring	antidote
discernible	cavorting	smoldering	fungus

HOW TO EAT FRIED WORMS

Discussion Questions

1 Which character did you like best? Why? (answers may vary)

2 Do you think the bet was fair? Why or why not? (answers may vary)

3 Joe and Alan tried many things to avoid losing the bet, from gluing two worms together to taking Billy to Shea Stadium and overfeeding him. Which of their ideas do you think was best? (answers may vary)

4 Billy prepared his worms in many different ways. Which "recipe" do you think sounded the best? (answers may vary)

5 Do you think it was a good idea for Joe and Alan to ask Billy's mother to be a referee when they went fishing? Why or why not? (answers may vary)

6 When do you think Alan first realized that he was going to lose the bet? (answers may vary)

7 Do you agree with Dr. McGrath that it was alright for Billy to eat worms? Why or why not? (answers may vary)

8 Who do you think was most responsible for Billy winning the bet? Why? (answers may vary)

Bulletin Board

Divide the bulletin board in half. Label one side "FOODS I LIKE LEAST" and the other side "FOODS I LIKE BEST." Ask students to draw or cut out pictures of two foods they like best and two foods they like least. Ask students to put their names on the pictures and then fasten them to the appropriate side of the bulletin board. Students may find out there are many similarities between their taste and other students' taste.

Name _____ Date _____

Directions

Below are arrows pointing between Billy and other characters in *How to Eat Fried Worms*. On the arrows pointing to Billy, write one word that describes how that character felt about Billy at the end of the book. On the arrows pointing away from Billy, write one word that tells how Billy felt about the other character at the end of the book.

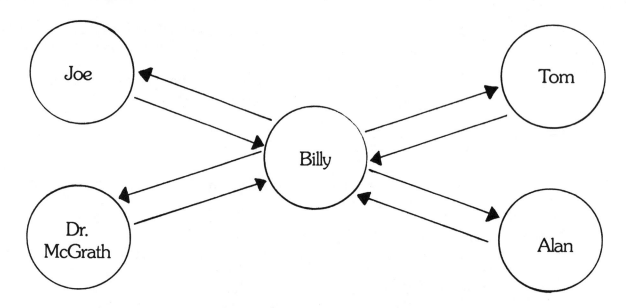

In the circle in the center of the diagram below, write your name. In the other circles write the names of friends or family members. Then follow the above directions to complete the diagram. You will have to imagine how each of the people named in the circles around your name feel about you.

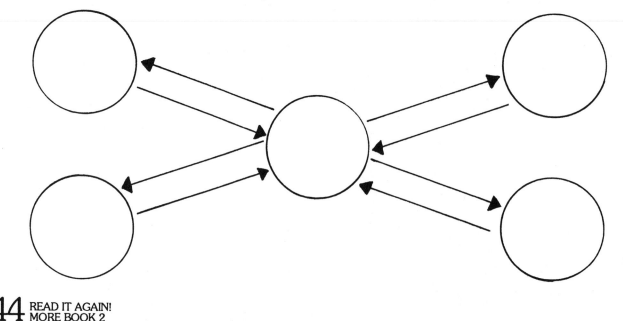

ACTIVITY
SHEET 2

Name _____ Date _____

Directions
In the spaces provided, list six things that you believe you would never eat.

_____   _____

_____   _____

_____   _____

In the book, Billy's mother suggests many ways to prepare worms: Creamed Worms on Toast, Spanish Worms, Wormloaf with Mushroom Sauce, and so on. Pretend that you are in a situation where you must eat four of the things you have listed above or suffer severe consequences. Create a recipe (with a name) that you think would be the best way to prepare each thing. Put your recipes in the boxes below.

Name _____ Date _____

Directions

Read each of the statements below and then decide if the characters should have behaved the way they did. Put a check in the worm under Agree if you agree with the way the character behaved and a check in the worm under Disagree if you don't agree with the way the character behaved. Finally, explain your answer.

**ACTIVITY
SHEET 3**

Agree   Disagree

1. Alan bet $50 that Billy could not eat fifteen worms. Do you think Alan should have made such a bet? Explain. _____

_____

2. Billy took Alan's bet to eat fifteen worms. Do you think Billy should have taken the bet? Explain. _____

_____

3. Alan agreed that Billy could prepare the worms any way he wanted. Do you think Alan should have made such an agreement? Explain. _____

_____

4. Alan glued two worms together and covered them with cornmeal so Billy would think he had one big worm. Do you think Alan should have done this? Explain. _____

_____

5. Alan asked Mrs. Forrester to make sure Billy ate his worm each day while Alan and Joe were gone. Do you think Alan should have asked Billy's mother to do this? Explain. _____

_____

6. Joe and Alan took Billy to Shea Stadium and fed him lots of food, hoping he'd fall asleep and forget to eat his worm. Do you think they should have done this? Explain. _____

_____

HOW TO EAT FRIED WORMS

Additional Activities

1 Ask each student to prepare a recipe for cooking worms. Next, combine the recipes to make a class cookbook titled [*teacher's name*] *Class Cookbook of Worms*.

Upon completion of the worm cookbook, have students agree on the recipe that sounds the most tasty. With help from students, collect all the ingredients needed to cook this recipe. Then cook a 16-ounce box of spaghetti, drain the spaghetti, add a tablespoon of cooking oil or margarine, and toss. Substituting the spaghetti for worms, provide students with time to prepare the recipe and eat it.

2 Instruct students to conduct a survey. Each should ask four people what food they dislike most. As a class project, list all the disliked foods and keep track of the times each is mentioned. If appropriate, graph the results. Students may discuss different ways to prepare foods to make them more palatable. For example, some people may not like creamed spinach but may like spinach salad.

3 The boys in the story argued about whether night crawlers are really worms. Assign students to research earthworms and prepare a brief report about them. Suggest they find out what earthworms eat, preferred types of habitat, their purpose, how they reproduce, and so on. The following books may be helpful and interesting:

> *Earthworms: Underground Farmers* by Patricia Lauber (Garrard, 1976)
>
> *Earthworms, Dirt, and Rotten Leaves: An Exploration in Ecology* by Molly McLaughlin (Atheneum, 1986)
>
> *Discovering What Earthworms Do* by Seymour Simon (McGraw-Hill, 1969)
>
> *The Amazing Earthworm* by Lilo Hess (Scribner's, 1979)

4 Obtain a gallon glass jar. As a class project, fill the jar with loose soil and some night crawlers. Observe what happens. Then ask students to write an imaginary story in which they accept a bet to eat the worms in the jar.

5 Encourage students to write sequels to the book *How to Eat Fried Worms*. Allow students time to share their sequels. Then obtain a copy of Thomas Rockwell's *How to Fight a Girl*, which is his sequel to *How to Eat Fried Worms*. Read *How to Fight a Girl* and discuss the similarities and differences between sequels.

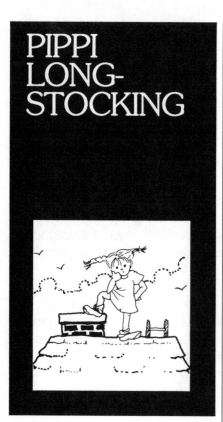

PIPPI LONG-STOCKING

Author
Astrid Lindgren

Illustrator
Louis S. Glanzman

Publisher
Viking, 1950

Pages	Reading Level	Interest Level
160	Gr. 4	Gr. 2–5

Other Books by Lindgren
Pippi Goes On Board; Pippi in the South Seas.

Information About the Author

Astrid Lindgren was born on November 14, 1907 near Vimmerby, Sweden, on a farm in an old red house with apple trees around it. Here she spent a childhood filled with security and freedom. She remembers her and her brother and sisters climbing like apes in trees and on roofs, crawling through tunnels, and swimming in rivers. They also worked in the fields, exchanging thoughts at the edge of the ditch during coffee breaks. Her introduction to books came when a girlfriend read her a fairy tale about the giant Bam Bam and the fairy Viribunda. When she learned to read, she asked for books for Christmas presents.

In school, her teachers predicted that Astrid Lindgren would become an author when she grew up. This prediction scared her so much that she decided she'd never write a book.

After completing school, she worked as a secretary, got married, and had two children. Throughout this time she told many stories but never wrote them down. When her seven-year-old daughter was ill, she kept asking her mother to tell her about Pippi Longstocking. For years Astrid Lindgren repeated the story. One day she sprained her ankle and was forced to stay in bed. To make time pass, she wrote Pippi stories in shorthand. She decided to write out the whole Pippi story and give the manuscript to her daughter as a tenth birthday present. She then sent a copy to a publisher.

This story, as well as others she wrote, became a success. She has been writing children's books since 1944, and they still appeal to young children. She continues to write and says that she writes to amuse the child within herself.

Summary

Pippi Longstocking lives in an old house in Villa Villekulla. She lives with a monkey named Mr. Nilsson and a horse. Her mother is an angel in heaven, and her father is a king on a cannibal island. Her next-door neighbors, Tommy and Annika, are her best friends. Together they experience many exciting adventures.

Introduction

In this story, Pippi lives on her own. Her mother is an angel in heaven, and her father is a king on a cannibal island. Would you like to be on your own? Why or why not?

Vocabulary Words

playmate	persuade	foreigner	cannibal
foliage	humiliating	promenade	injustice
commands	astonishment	radiant	courageous
disdainfully	expedition	innocent	

PIPPI LONGSTOCKING

Discussion Questions

1 Describe Pippi's appearance. (answers may vary)

2 Would you like to have Pippi living next to you? Why or why not ? (answers may vary)

3 Pippi tells many stories. Which story was your favorite? (answers may vary)

4 Describe some of the things Pippi did at Mrs. Settergren's coffee party. How do you feel about her behavior? (answers may vary)

5 Have you ever been to a birthday party like Pippi's? If so, how was it the same? If not, how was it different? (answers may vary)

6 Tommy and Annika do many things with Pippi. What do you think they did with her that was the funniest? The scariest? The most exciting? (answers may vary)

7 What do you think Pippi will do when she grows up? (answers may vary)

8 Would you read another Pippi Longstocking adventure? Why or why not? (answers may vary)

Bulletin Board

Give each student a paper plate. Have students create Pippi's face on the paper plates. Remind them that she has a nose the shape of a small potato, freckles, a wide mouth, and white teeth. For her hair, give them red yarn to create two braids, which they can glue to their paper plate. Attach the Pippi paper plates to the bulletin board. Label the bulletin board "PIPPI LONGSTOCKING."

PIPPI LONGSTOCKING

ACTIVITY SHEET 1

Directions
Create Pippi Longstocking by following the directions. As you read each direction and complete it, check it off.

1. ☐ Draw two straight braids that stick out.
2. ☐ Color her hair the color of a carrot.
3. ☐ Draw her nose the shape of a small potato.
4. ☐ Dot her nose with freckles.
5. ☐ Draw her mouth wide.
6. ☐ Draw strong white teeth.
7. ☐ Draw a dress on Pippi. Color it blue and red.
8. ☐ Draw long, thin legs.
9. ☐ Draw stockings on Pippi's legs. Color one brown and one black.
10. ☐ Draw big shoes on Pippi. Color them black.

From *Read It Again! More Book 2* published by GoodYearBooks. Copyright © 1991 Liz Rothlein and Terri Christman.

**ACTIVITY
SHEET 2**

Name _____ Date _____

Directions

Pretend you are Pippi, the thing finder. In the box below, Pippi started to draw something she found. Complete the drawing, and answer the following questions.

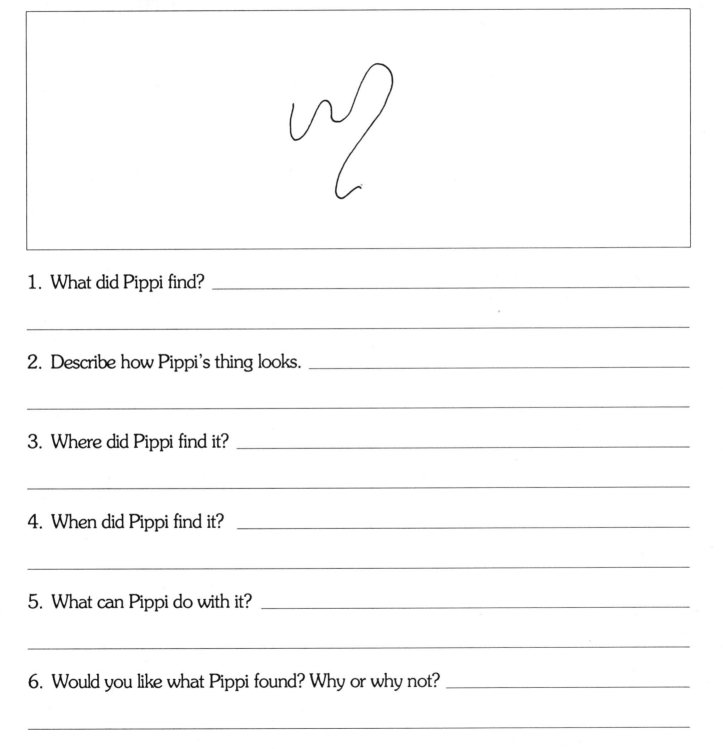

1. What did Pippi find? _____

_____

2. Describe how Pippi's thing looks. _____

_____

3. Where did Pippi find it? _____

_____

4. When did Pippi find it? _____

_____

5. What can Pippi do with it? _____

_____

6. Would you like what Pippi found? Why or why not? _____

_____

From *Read It Again! More Book 2* published by GoodYearBooks. Copyright © 1991 Liz Rothlein and Terri Christman.

PIPPI LONGSTOCKING

ACTIVITY SHEET 3

Directions

Answer the following questions in complete sentences.

1. How does Pippi, nine years old, feel about living in an old house in Villa Villekulla all alone? _____

_____

How would you feel? _____

_____

2. How does Pippi handle the five boys beating up Willie? _____

_____

What would you do? _____

_____

3. What does Pippi do when the police come to her house? _____

_____

What would you do? _____

_____

4. How does Pippi behave in school? _____

_____

How would you behave? _____

_____

5. Why does Pippi climb down into the hollow tree? _____

_____

What would you do? _____

_____

6. How does Pippi clean her floors? _____

_____

How would you do it? _____

_____

7. What does Pippi do at the circus? _____

_____

What would you do? _____

_____

8. What does Pippi do with the burglars? _____

_____

What would you do with burglars? _____

_____

9. How does Pippi rescue two boys from a burning building? _____

_____

What would you do? _____

_____

10. How does Pippi celebrate her birthday? _____

_____

How do you celebrate your birthday? _____

_____

From *Read It Again! More Book 2* published by GoodYearBooks. Copyright © 1991 Liz Rothlein and Terri Christman.

Additional Activities

1   Talk to students about the Sunday afternoon the quiet little town of Villa Villekulla was filled with excitement due to a fire. A building, called "the skyscraper" because it was so tall, was burning. Two boys were caught in the burning building, but Pippi rescued them. Invite a fire fighter in to talk to students about how he or she became a fire fighter, his or her duties, procedures students should follow if they are in a burning building, and so on.

2   Ask students to think about having Pippi for a friend. Have them fold a piece of paper in half lengthwise and label one column "Positive" and one column "Negative." Have them individually list as many responses as possible under each column. Then divide students into small groups to share and add to their lists. Finally, discuss the lists with the entire class.

3   Have students list all the places Pippi says she has been (Egypt, Congo, Brazil, Borneo, Portugal, India, Argentina, and China) and locate them on a map. Discuss what Pippi said about each place, how she might have traveled to each location, and so on. Perhaps you can assign students to research these places and share their information with the rest of the class.

4   Pippi did a great deal of cooking. She learned cooking from the cook on her father's ship. She made pancakes, Swedish cookies, buns, meatball and ham sandwiches, pineapple pudding, and other things. Provide the following ingredients, and allow time for the class to make the recipe:

Pippi's Pineapple Cream Tarts

Tart Shells: 1 cup of butter or magarine
1 cup of cottage cheese
2 cups of all-purpose flour
2 tablespoons of cinnamon

Cream together the cottage cheese and butter. Add the flour and cinnamon. Roll into small balls and place in miniature muffin cups. Shape around the inside of each cup. Bake 20 minutes at 350 degrees. Cool, remove shells from muffin pans, and fill with Pippi's pineapple cream filling.

Pineapple Cream Filling: 8-ounce package of cream cheese
small can of crushed pineapple
1/3 cup of finely crushed walnuts

Mix cream cheese and pineapple together. Add nuts. Put mixture into tart shells.

---

5   Show the movie *Pippi Longstocking* to your class. As a group, discuss how the movie and book differ. Have students decide which one they like best and tell why in paragraph form. Share the paragraphs aloud.

6   In the story, Pippi tells her teacher her name is Pippilotta Delicatessa Windowshade Mackrelmint Efraim's Daughter Longstocking. Ask your students to write a funny name for themselves. Share their names with the entire class.

From *Read It Again! More Book 2* published by GoodYearBooks. Copyright © 1991 Liz Rothlein and Terri Christman.

RENT A THIRD GRADER

Author
B. B. Hiller

Illustrator
Meredith Johnson

Publisher
Scholastic, 1988

Pages 190	Reading Level Gr. 4	Interest Level Gr. 3–6

Other Books by Hiller
Karate Kid; Karate Kid: II

Information About the Author
No information available.

Summary
Partner, a police department horse, is going to be sold to the HappiPet Food Company to be turned into pet food. A class of third-grade students want to raise enough money to board Partner at Akers Acres for the rest of his life. They come up with the Rent a Third Grader idea to raise the money.

Introduction
This is a story about how the students in a third-grade class work *together* to save a horse. Have you ever worked together with others to accomplish something? If so, for what? Could you have done it by yourself? Why or why not?

Vocabulary Words

rent	majestically	camouflaged	contradicted
sauntering	cooperated	patiently	vaguely
masterminded	ridiculous	loped	nutritious
wailing	drenching	guaranteed	

RENT A THIRD GRADER

Discussion Questions

1 Have you ever had to give an oral report? If so, how did you feel about it? (answers may vary)

2 Why did the students feel they needed to save Partner? (answers may vary)

3 How do the students advertise Rent a Third Grader? What are some other ways they could advertise? (ad in the *PennySaver*, posters; answers may vary)

4 Describe Akers Acres. (answers may vary)

5 Discuss some of the failures the students had while trying to raise money. Why didn't they give up? (car wash, paper drive, cookie sale, and so on; answers may vary)

6 In the story, Brad makes a list of things he doesn't want to think about: the HappiPet Food Company, the bill from Akers Acres, the cookie sale, the paper drive, the car wash, dogs, and $18.76. What would your list be? (answers may vary)

7 How did the class trip to Akers Acres help the Rent a Third Grader business boom? (answers may vary)

8 At the end of the story, the Rent a Third Grader business is going to make a lot of money. The students begin to think of other ways to use the money in their community. If your class raised money for your community, what would it be used for? (answers may vary)

Bulletin Board

The students in Miss Bilgore's class advertise the Rent a Third Grader business in the *PennySaver*. Have students cut out newspaper ads describing services that are available. Place the ads into categories, such as secretarial and accounting. Label the bulletin board with these categories and staple ads where they belong. The bulletin board will be a collage of ads. Label it "DO YOU NEED A . . .?"

From *Read It Again! More Book 2* published by GoodYearBooks. Copyright © 1991 Liz Rothlein and Terri Christman.

RENT A THIRD
GRADER

ACTIVITY
SHEET 1

Directions
After looking at each picture, fill in the blank telling who it is and
what he or she is doing. The characters' names are in the box.

| Miss Bilgore | Officer Chambliss | Partner | Brad | Louisa | Jenny |

1. This is _____.

   He/she is _____

   _____.

2. This is _____.

   He/she is _____

   _____.

3. This is _____.

   He/she is _____

   _____.

4. This is _____.

   He/she is _____

   _____.

5. This is _____.

   He/she is _____

   _____.

6. This is _____.

   He/she is _____

   _____.

From *Read It Again! More Book 2* published by GoodYearBooks. Copyright © 1991 Liz Rothlein and Terri Christman.

Name _____ Date _____

**ACTIVITY
SHEET 2**

Directions
Read the description of each character and match it with the
appropriate character. The first one is done for you.

___d___ 1. Brad

_____ 2. Miss Bilgore

_____ 3. Jennie

_____ 4. Officer Chambliss

_____ 5. Partner

_____ 6. Louisa

_____ 7. Mr. Mustache (Rodney Snodgrass)

_____ 8. Mr. Akers

_____ 9. Mr. Costello

_____ 10. Ellie

_____ 11. Jeremy

_____ 12. Zoe

a. He showed the kids the pasture where Partner would graze.
b. She walked Charlie (Mrs. Tooker's dog).
c. She made posters.
d. He didn't want to give his social studies report.
e. She wanted to have a paper drive.
f. She was a third-grade teacher.
g. He tried to get Partner in the HappiPet Food Company truck.
h. Mrs. Chessman wanted her to babysit.
i. He raked leaves for Mrs. Atherton.
j. He wanted Brad to help him store and catalog his baseball cards.
k. The children fed him carrots, lumps of sugar, and apples.
l. He was the afternoon crossing guard.

Who was your favorite character? _____

Explain. _____

_____

_____

_____

RENT A THIRD GRADER

Name _____ Date _____

Directions

Pretend your class is trying to earn money. Complete the information about yourself below. In the box, draw something to represent your service.

Rent a _____ Grader

(your grade level)

Name: _____

Description of yourself: _____

_____

_____

_____

Service you could provide: _____

_____

Hours available: _____

Charge: _____

RENT A THIRD GRADER

Additional Activities

1 As a class, discuss the cookie sale that was suppose to take place in the story. Have students discuss what Louisa did, what she didn't do, how Brad and Jenny treated her, and how disappointed the students were because there was no bake sale. Then try this recipe in class. Instead of selling the cookies, eat them and enjoy.

No-Bake Cookies

2 cups of sugar
½ cup of milk
⅓ cup of butter
1 teaspoon of vanilla
½ teaspoon of salt

Mix these ingredients together and bring to a boil. Remove from heat and add the following ingredients.

3 cups of quick-cook oats
⅓ cup of cocoa
½ cup of peanut butter

Drop by the tablespoon on wax paper. Yields approximately forty cookies.

---

2 Invite into the classroom a police officer who rides a horse while on duty. Ask him or her to discuss the pros and cons of riding a horse instead of using a car, motorcycle, helicopter, or other vehicle. Discuss the training involved, the care, and so on. Perhaps the horse can also visit the school.

3 Have students list things they could buy for their community. Decide as a group the cost of each and the one they would like to try raising money for. Next, have them list ways they could make money. For example, the students in the story have a car wash, a cookie sale, and a paper drive and rake leaves, babysit, and water plants. Perhaps students can try one of the ideas and see what they can do for their community.

4 Chapter 31 in *Rent a Third Grader* is called "The End—Or Is It?" Discuss this title with students. Talk about why Partner won't be needing the money anymore and what the students are thinking about doing with the money they raised. Have students write and title a Chapter 32, which should tell what jobs the students in the story continue to get and what their community project is going to be. Share the final chapters aloud.

5 Have students create individual lists of all the things they would see on a farm. Have them share their lists. Take a field trip to a farm. It might be a good idea to have students list some questions they want to ask before they go. After they return, have them check their lists of things they thought they would see on the farm. Have them create and illustrate a paragraph describing their experience. Share the projects with the class.

STUART LITTLE

Author
E. B. White

Illustrator
Garth Williams

Publisher
Dell, 1945

Pages 138	Reading Level Gr. 4	Interest Level Gr. 2–5

Other Books by White
Charlotte's Web; Trumpet of the Swan

Information About the Author

E. B. White was born on July 11, 1899 in Mt. Vernon, New York. His father was a piano manufacturer. E. B. White married an editor and had one child. He once said that he knew he had married the right woman when once they were packing and she said to be sure to put in the tooth twine. He said that anyone who called dental floss tooth twine was right for him.

As an adult, E. B. White moved to a farm in North Brooklin, Maine. On that farm he got the idea to write *Charlotte's Web.* One day when he was in the barn feeding his pig, he began feeling sorry for it, because he knew it was doomed to die. Thinking of ways to save the pig, he came up with the idea of *Charlotte's Web,* which won a Newbery Honor Award in 1953.

In addition to writing books for children, E. B. White wrote books for adults. He also was a contributing editor to *The New Yorker* and wrote a monthly column for *Harper's* magazine. In 1963 he was named by President John F. Kennedy as one of thirty-eight Americans to receive the Presidential Medal of Freedom. E. B. White died in October 1985 of Alzheimer's disease.

Summary

Stuart Little is the second son born to Mr. and Mrs. Little. He looks like a mouse. He is about 2 inches tall and has a tail, a pointed nose, and whiskers. Because of his small size, he is very helpful at home. Everyone in the family loves Stuart.

One day Stuart's mother rescues a bird named Margalo. Stuart and Margalo become very good friends. However, Margalo learns that a neighbor's cat is going to eat her. She leaves without telling anyone. Stuart sets out to find her. His adventures along the way are quite exciting and interesting.

Introduction

In this story, Mr. and Mrs. Little (human beings) have two sons, George and Stuart (a mouse). If you were George, how would you feel about having a brother who's a mouse?

Vocabulary Words

shy	infant	belittling	solemnly
shrill	vigorous	sorrow	contented
inquired	gazing	modestly	promptly
prominent	souvenir	peered	

STUART LITTLE

Discussion Questions

1 Describe Stuart Little's appearance. (he looked like a mouse, with a mouse's sharp nose, a mouse's tail, and a mouse's whiskers)

2 Would you like to be 2 inches tall? Why or why not? (answers may vary)

3 Describe some of the helpful things Stuart did around the house. (answers may vary but might include retrieving a ring that had fallen down a drain, helping George play the piano, and helping retrieve the ball during ping-pong games)

4 Explain how Stuart ended up on a garbage scow. (answers may vary)

5 Why did Margalo leave? (answers may vary but might include because she was frightened, because of the note warning her of the cat, or because it was springtime and birds fly north)

6 Stuart decided to look for Margalo . What did he pack in his handkerchief? If you were going out to find someone, what would you pack? (toothbrush, money, soap, comb, brush, clean suit of underwear, pocket compass, and a strand of Mrs. Little's hair; answers may vary)

7 Stuart had several adventures while looking for Margalo. Which adventure did you enjoy the most? Why? (answers may vary)

8 Do you think Stuart ever found Margalo? Explain. (answers may vary)

Bulletin Board
Place the caption "[teacher's name] LITTLE CLASS" on the bulletin board. Tell students to pretend they were born small like Stuart Little. Provide each student with a copy of the form on page 64 and ask them to fill it out. Display their completed projects on the bulletin board.

_____ Little

[student's first name]

Illustration of how small I am:

I like being little because _____

_____

_____

_____

I do not like being little because _____

_____

_____

_____

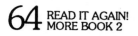

Name _____ Date _____

**ACTIVITY
SHEET 1**

Directions
Read all the words in the outline of Stuart. On the worksheet on page 66, list each word with the correct adventure. Add some of your own words. Then choose the adventure you like best. Using the words, describe the adventure in paragraph form in the space below.

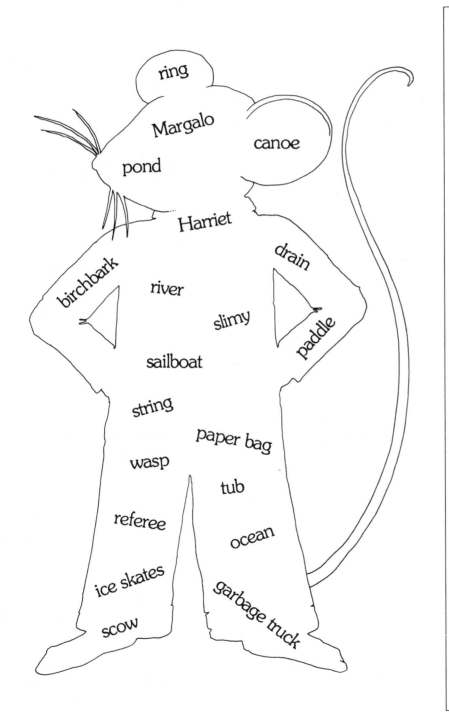

ring

Margalo

canoe

pond

Harriet

birchbark

river

drain

slimy

paddle

sailboat

string

paper bag

wasp

tub

referee

ocean

ice skates

garbage truck

scow

1. _____

_____

_____

_____

_____

_____

_____

2. _____

_____

_____

_____

_____

_____

_____

3. _____

_____

_____

_____

_____

_____

_____

4. _____

_____

_____

_____

_____

_____

_____

From *Read It Again! More Book 2* published by GoodYearBooks. Copyright © 1991 Liz Rothlein and Terri Christman.

| Name _____ Date _____

Directions
A thank you note should include the date, the greeting, the paragraph, the closing, and the signature. Fill in the missing information below using the names in the box. Then select a situation below and create a thank you note. Be sure all five parts of a thank you note appear.

Margalo	superintendent	Stuart	George
Mrs. Little	Dr. Paul Carey	pigeon	

Who is thanking?	Whom are they thanking?	Thanking for what?
1. Stuart		rescued from the garbage scow
2.	Stuart	got the ring out of the drain
3.	Mr. Little	made him a tiny bed
4. the Littles		chased ping-pong balls
5.	Stuart	pushed the piano key up when it played
6.	George	pulled the shade down
7. Dr. Paul Carey		won the sailboat race
8. the Littles		brought Stuart home
9. Margalo		wrote a warning letter
10. Stuart		gave him an automobile
11.	Stuart	taught for Miss Gunderson
12. Harriet		invited her to ride in a canoe

| Name _____ Date _____

ACTIVITY SHEET 3

Directions
The last sentence in *Stuart Little* lets us know that Stuart continues his search for Margalo. Create a final chapter, Chapter 16. Answering the following questions may help you write your final chapter.

Does Stuart find Margalo? _____

If not, what does Stuart do? _____

If so, where does he find her? _____

What is she doing? _____

Did she miss Stuart? _____

Does she want to come back? _____

Does he bring her back? _____

Is she safe at the Littles' house? _____

Were the Littles worried about Stuart being gone? _____

What other adventures does Stuart have in Chapter 16? _____

_____

_____

_____

_____

_____

_____

Continue your chapter on additional sheets of paper.

From *Read It Again! More Book 2* published by GoodYearBooks. Copyright © 1991 Liz Rothlein and Terri Christman.

STUART LITTLE

Additional Activities

1 Talk to students about Stuart's size (2 inches high). Discuss some of the things the Littles did to make Stuart's life easier. Some examples: Mr. Little made him a tiny bed out of four clothespins and a cigarette box; Mrs. Little tied a long string to the pull chain of a light; Mr. Little fixed a tiny rope ladder to the washbasin; Mrs. Little gave him a doll-size toothbrush, soap, washcloth, and comb. Have each student create a home for Stuart out of a shoe box. Be creative!

2 Discuss and define the terms "reality" and "fantasy" with students. Next, have them orally give some examples of each. Then give them each a piece of writing paper. Have them fold it in half lengthwise, writing the word "reality" on one side and the word "fantasy" on the other. Give students a few minutes on their own to place events from the story under each column heading. Then get together as a class and share the lists. Allow students to add to their lists any of the events they hear.

3 Discuss with students the pros and cons of being small like Stuart. Have them think of things they could do if they were small and things they couldn't do if they were small. Finally, have them take a stand: Would they want to be small or not? Once they have decided, have them explain why or why not in paragraph form and then share their paragraphs.

4 Invite a person from a nearby pet store to bring a mouse or mice to your classroom. Ask him or her to talk to students about what mice eat, their care, and the like. Provide time for questions. Students may want to have their questions prepared ahead of time. After the presenter leaves, list as a class, on chart paper or on the chalkboard, all the facts they have learned about mice. Perhaps the pet store would donate a mouse and cage to your classroom.

5 Discuss with students Stuart and Margalo's special friendship. Stuart is very determined to find Margalo. He experiences a great deal while looking for her. Have students talk about some of the special things they have done for their best friends. Also discuss why they did these special things.

6 As a class project, make a bird feeder that may attract birds. For each feeder, purchase ½ pound suet from a meat or butcher shop, a 12 × 12 inch piece of netting, and birdseed. Roll the suet in the birdseed, and then place the seeded suet in the netting. Tie the corners of the netting together and hang it in a tree or on an outside windowsill, so students can watch the birds feed.

THE BORROWERS

Author
Mary Norton

Illustrators
Beth and Joe Krush

Publisher
Harcourt, 1952

Pages	Reading Level	Interest Level
180	Gr. 5	Gr. 3–7

Other Books by Norton
The Borrowers Afield; The Borrowers Afloat; The Borrowers Aloft; The Borrowers Avenged; Bed-Knob and Broomstick; Poor Stainless; Are All the Giants Dead?

Information About the Author
Mary Norton was born on December 10, 1903 in London, England. She was married and had four children. She started out being an actress, which was actually her first love. She and her family moved a lot. She lived in Portugal, England, New York, and Horta in the Azores.

Mary Norton started writing in 1947. She became well known for her Borrowers series, stories about a family of 6-inch-high people who hide in the houses of human beings. These stories Mary Norton attributes to her childhood days in the countryside of Leighton Buzzard. As a child she often lingered, stared, and investigated her environment. She was very imaginative as well as rebellious.

Summary
Pod and Homily Clock and their daughter Arrietty, the Borrowers, live in a quiet old country house in England. They are small people living under the floor of Great-Aunt Sophy's house. They are very good at borrowing things from Great-Aunt Sophy, but they are always afraid of being seen by human beings. One day Pod takes Arrietty, his daughter, borrowing. She meets a boy who is staying with his Great-Aunt Sophy. A unique friendship begins, and many exciting events follow.

Introduction
This story helps explain where things go when we can't find them. The Borrowers (little people living under the floor of the house) borrow things and place them in their home under the floor. What have you lost at your house? Do you think the Borrowers live at your house?

Vocabulary Words

generation	deny	deliberate	ancestors
passage	tentatively	dusk	dismayed
stealthily	fortress	astounded	ventilation
threshold	trench		

THE BORROWERS

Discussion Questions

1 Which character did you like best? Explain. (answers may vary)

2 Describe how Arrietty felt about the way she and her family lived. (answers may vary)

3 Why do you think Homily and Pod decided to allow Arrietty to go borrowing? (answers may vary)

4 What were some of the nice things the boy did for the Borrowers? What were some of the nice things the Borrowers did for the boy? (answers may vary)

5 Look up the definitions of "borrow" and "steal." Arrietty calls what she does borrowing, and the boy calls it stealing. What do you think the Borrowers are doing? (answers may vary)

6 Decide how Mrs. Driver found the Borrowers. (answers may vary)

7 What do you have at your house that a Borrower might want? (answers may vary)

8 What would you like and dislike about being a Borrower? (answers may vary)

Bulletin Board

Label the bulletin board "[teacher's name] BORROWERS." Give each student a copy of page 72 to complete. Tell them to pretend they are Borrowers. They will need to decide what one item they would borrow from their own house, where they would find it, and how they would use it. Finally, they will need to illustrate that object in use. Post students' papers on the bulletin board when they are finished.

Name _____

```
┌─────────────────────────────────────────────────┐
│                                                 │
│                                                 │
│                                                 │
│                                                 │
│                                                 │
│                                                 │
│                                                 │
│                                                 │
│                                                 │
│                                                 │
│                                                 │
│                                                 │
│                                                 │
└─────────────────────────────────────────────────┘
```

If I were a Borrower, I would borrow a/an _____.

I would find it in the _____.

I would use it _____

_____

_____.

THE BORROWERS

Name _____ Date _____

Directions

After completing *The Borrowers*, decide which part was the funniest, happiest, saddest, scariest, bravest, and best. Then illustrate each part in the space provided.

1. The funniest part was _____

_____

_____

2. The happiest part was _____

_____

_____

3. The saddest part was _____

_____

_____

4. The scariest part was _____

_____

_____

5. The bravest part was _____

_____

_____

6. The best part was _____

_____

_____

THE BORROWERS

Name _____ Date _____

Directions
Below are some of the characters from *The Borrowers*. Describe each one or tell something he or she did in the story.

Mrs. May _____

_____

Kate _____

_____

Mrs. May's brother _____

_____

Pod _____

_____

Homily _____

_____

Arrietty _____

_____

Mrs. Driver _____

_____

Great-Aunt Sophy _____

_____

Crampfurl _____

_____

From *Read It Again! More Book 2* published by GoodYearBooks. Copyright © 1991 Liz Rothlein and Terri Christman.

THE
BORROWERS

Name _____ Date _____

Directions
Complete the following chart showing causes and effects.

Cause	Effect
1. Kate lost her crochet hook.	
2.	He was sent to live in the country with his Great-Aunt Sophy.
3. Arrietty went down the path to the bank.	
4.	Homily suggested that Pod take Arrietty borrowing.
5. The boy delivered Arrietty's letter down the hole.	
6. Arrietty read to the boy.	
7.	Mrs. Driver wrenched back the piece of floor and saw little people.
8. Write another cause and effect from *The Borrowers*, and illustrate your choice.	

THE BORROWERS

Additional Activities

1 As a group, have students come up with a list of small things they might find in a house. Have them copy this list. Next, give each student a sheet of 11 × 14 inch white paper. Have them draw a home for the Borrowers, using the items on their list. Allow students time to share and explain their drawings.

2 Create a column on the chalkboard titled "Why I wouldn't want to be a Borrower" and one titled "Why I would like to be a Borrower." As a group, have students add things to both columns. Discuss the lists, and then ask students to decide whether they would or would not like to be a Borrower. Then have students develop a paragraph supporting their decision. Have them share their paragraphs aloud with the group.

3 Discuss the ending of *The Borrowers* with your students. Talk about how it leaves you wondering. For example, was that really a teapot Mrs. May found? Who took the pillowcase? Whose hotpot was Mrs. May smelling? Whose writing was in the Memoranda? Have your students create a Chapter 21 to give the book a more final ending. Share their final chapters aloud.

From *Read It Again! More Book 2* published by GoodYearBooks. Copyright © 1991 Liz Rothlein and Terri Christman.

FANTASTIC MR. FOX

Author
Roald Dahl

Illustrator
Donald Chaffin

Publisher
Knopf, 1970

Pages 62	Reading Level Gr. 5	Interest Level Gr. 3–6

Other Books by Dahl
James and the Giant Peach;
Charlie and the Chocolate
Factory; The Magic Finger

Information About the Author
Roald Dahl (pronounced Roo-all) was born on September 13, 1916 in Llandoff, South Wales. He had three children. He was a freelance writer and served in the military. Later, only as a result of reading stories to his own children, he became interested in writing children's books. He rarely found any books that really excited his children, so he decided to tell them his own stories, which he then made into books. He lived in Buckinghamshire, England, until his death in November 1990.

Summary
Each day Mr. Fox brings home food for his family (chickens, ducks, geese, turkeys) from one of three farms. The farmers decide they are going to get Mr. Fox. They try to dig up the fox family's hole using shovels and tractors. The farmers think they will starve out the foxes. Instead, Mr. Fox digs tunnels to each of the farms and gathers food not only for his family but also for his friends, so they never have to come out of their holes again.

Introduction
This story is called *Fantastic Mr. Fox*. As you listen to this story, you will hear why the fox is called Fantastic. Do you have a nickname? What is it? How did you get that nickname?

Vocabulary Words
farmer	fantastic	reeks	enormous
crouched	desperate	prowling	jeers
obstinate	wafted	chortle	chaos
dwarf	feast	ravenous	

FANTASTIC MR. FOX

Discussion Questions

1 Why did the three farmers want to kill Mr. Fox and his family? (Mr. Fox was taking their food away from them)

2 What would you do to stop Mr. Fox from stealing your food? (answers may vary)

3 Describe all three farmers. Tell how they were alike and how they were different. (answers may vary)

4 Why did the farmers help one another try to catch Mr. Fox? (they didn't want anything stolen anymore)

5 Why were the badger, mole, rabbit, and weasel upset with Mr. Fox? (they couldn't get out of their holes, and they were starving)

6 At the end of the story, Boggis, Bunce, and Bean are waiting by the hole for the fox to come out. If you were the farmers, how long would you wait? What would you do next? (answers may vary)

7 Do you think Mr. Fox is fantastic? Why or why not? (answers may vary)

8 How does the author make the animals seem like people? (answers may vary)

Bulletin Board

Place the caption "FANTASTIC HAPPENINGS" on the bulletin board. Have students create a paragraph describing something fantastic they have done. Have them also create an illustration that represents their paragraph. The title of their paragraph should include their name: "Fantastic Mr./Miss _____."
Share the projects aloud before displaying them on the bulletin board.

From *Read It Again! More Book 2* published by GoodYearBooks. Copyright © 1991 Liz Rothlein and Terri Christman.

Name _____ Date _____

Directions

Below are descriptions of some of the characters in *Fantastic Mr. Fox*. The characters' names are in the box. After you have read each description, place the character's name on the blank line. Create a picture of the character in the box.

Mr. Fox	Boggis	Mr. Badger	Bean	Rat	Bunce

1. This character is a chicken farmer. He keeps thousands of chickens. He is enormous. He eats three boiled chickens smothered with dumplings every day, for breakfast, lunch, and dinner. Who is he? _____

2. This character is very clever. Each night he creeps down into the valley in the darkness of night and helps himself to the farmers' food. Who is he?

_____

3. This character is a turkey and apple farmer. He keeps thousands of turkeys in an orchard full of apple trees. He doesn't eat food. However, he does drink gallons of strong cider. He is thin and clever. Who is he? _____

4. This character has a small sharp face with whiskers. He lives in Mr. Bean's cellar. He drinks cider. Who is he? _____

5. This character is a duck and goose farmer. He keeps thousands of ducks and geese. He is a kind of pot-bellied dwarf. He mashes goose livers into paste and stuffs it into doughnuts. Who is he? _____

6. This character has a deep voice. He has a long, black, pointed, funny face. He helps Mr. Fox gather food for the others. Who is he? _____

ACTIVITY
SHEET 2

Directions
Some things in *Fantastic Mr. Fox* could happen in real life. Some things could not happen. Read the following list of events that happened in the story. Write the things that could happen in Column 1. Write the things that could not happen in Column 2.

The animals never going outside
Foxes living in a hole
Mr. Fox talking to his family
Farmers shooting a fox
The animals having a feast at a table
The badger worrying about "stealing"
The foxes eating chickens

The farmers still waiting today for Mr. Fox
Using a mechanical shovel to dig a hole
People laughing at the farmers
Mrs. Fox getting weak from lack of food
   and water
A rat sucking cider through a tube

Column 1
Things That Could Happen

Column 2
Things That Could Not Happen

From *Read It Again! More Book 2* published by GoodYearBooks. Copyright © 1991 Liz Rothlein and Terri Christman.

Name _____ Date _____

Directions

Below is a list of animals in *Fantastic Mr. Fox*. Using an encyclopedia, fill in the missing information.

Name of Animal	Appearance	Food	Habitat	Enemies
Fox				
Rat				
Weasel				
Badger				
Mole				
Animal of Your Choice _____				

Draw a picture of your favorite animal in its habitat on the back of this page.

FANTASTIC MR. FOX

Additional Activities

1 Discuss with students how they feel about Mr. Fox taking food from the farmers. Was the fox "stealing"? Was he right in doing it to keep his family and friends from starving to death? Have students take a stand. Ask them to create a paragraph supporting their choice. Share their writings with the class. Be sure to tally the votes.

2 Discuss with students the term "personify." Talk about how Roald Dahl personifies the animals in this story. Have students come up with a list of other books where the animals are personified. Have them try to write their own stories personifying an animal. Share the stories aloud.

3 Place the name of each character in *Fantastic Mr. Fox* on a piece of paper: Mr. Fox, Bunce, Mr. Badger, Rat, Mrs. Fox, Mrs. Bean, Bean, Boggis, Mabel. Place the papers in a container. Allow a student to draw out one paper, read the name silently, and then use gestures and facial expressions to reveal the character (as in charades). The student who guesses correctly gets to draw the next paper.

4 Invite a farmer into your classroom to speak to students. Ask the farmer to talk about his or her duties, the crops raised on the farm, which animals are a nuisance, what a typical day is like for him, and so on. Perhaps students could each write a question on a small piece of paper before the farmer comes in.

5 Tape a large sheet of white paper on your chalkboard (enough to cover it). Have students draw or paint a picture of the animals' underground homes (badgers, weasels, foxes, rabbits, moles). The students might also want to depict the three farms above the ground. They could also add the cider cellar. Once the picture is complete, label all the parts. Display it on a wall in the classroom.

From *Read It Again! More Book 2* published by GoodYearBooks. Copyright © 1991 Liz Rothlein and Terri Christman.

ISLAND OF THE BLUE DOLPHINS

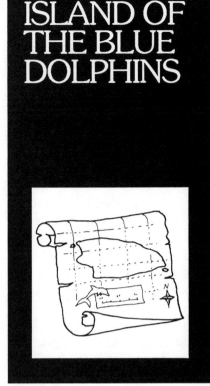

Author
Scott O'Dell

Publisher
Dell, 1960

Pages 184	Reading Level Gr. 5	Interest Level Gr. 4–7

Other Books by O'Dell
The Kings Fifth; The Black Pearl; Zia; The Dark Canoe; The Spanish Smile; Journey to Jericho; Sing Down the Moon; Kathleen, Please Come Home; Sarah Bishop

Information About the Author
Scott O'Dell was born in 1903 on what was later called Terminal Island near Los Angeles, California. Throughout his boyhood, he lived near the sea. He has worked in the motion picture industry, as a book reviewer, and as a newspaper journalist. He also wrote fiction and nonfiction articles for periodicals and books for young people.

Scott O'Dell's first book, *Island of the Blue Dolphins*, was based on a true story about a young Indian girl who lived alone on an island for many years. This book won the Newbery Award, the Rupert Hughes Award, the German Juvenile International Award, and the William Allen White Award.

Summary
Karana, a young girl, has lived alone for years on an island in the Pacific. She waits year after year, season after season, for her people to come in a ship and take her away. While she waits she keeps herself alive by finding whatever food is available and by building herself a shelter. As she struggles to stay alive, she makes weapons to help protect herself from a pack of wild dogs. This is an adventure of survival that portrays courage and greatness of spirit.

Introduction
This is a story about a young girl who was left to live alone on an island in the Pacific Ocean. She not only had to provide food, clothing, and shelter for herself but also had to protect herself from a pack of wild dogs. How do you think you would react if you found yourself in a similar situation?

Vocabulary Words

ravine	carcass	vanquished	sinews
gorge	prey	lair	reproachfully
omen	faggot	stalking	fledglings
cormorants			

Discussion Questions

1 Why do you think Karana's father gave his real name, which is usually secret, instead of his common name to the stranger in the boat? (answers may vary)

2 The sea otter and the seal look alike when they are swimming, but they are very different. What are the differences? (otter has shorter nose, small webbed feet instead of flippers, thicker fur that is more beautiful)

3 What kind of leader do you think Karana's father was? (answers may vary)

4 How did Karana feel about killing otters? Explain the viewpoint of Karana's father. (angry because she liked watching the otters and they were her friends; he said there were plenty of otters and they would come back when the hunters left)

5 When given the opportunity, why were the villagers of Ghalas-at so willing to leave their island after the fight with the Aleuts? (because they had many bad memories of the dead)

6 Why do you think Karana couldn't kill the leader of the wild dogs even though she had planned to and had the opportunity to do so? How do you think Karana would have felt if she had killed the dog? (answers may vary)

7 Why do you think Karana and Tutok befriended each other despite their anxieties and the risks involved? (answers may vary)

8 Karana lived alone on the Island of the Blue Dolphins for 18 years. During this time, she showed strength and resourcefulness. Do you think she would have been this strong and resourceful if she had lived with the people of her village? Why or why not? (answers may vary)

Bulletin Board

Tell students to pretend they are travel agents and have just discovered the Island of the Blue Dolphins. Ask each of them to fold a 9 × 12 inch sheet of paper into three sections, as shown here. Tell students to use this folded sheet of paper to

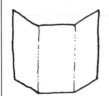

make a travel brochure that would make people want to visit this island. Include such information as cost of the trip, type of transportation, weather information, facilities that are available (hotels, motels, restaurants, parks, and so forth), things to do on the island, illustrations and pictures of the island.

After the brochures have been completed, fasten them to the bulletin board. Title the bulletin board "WE ARE OFF TO THE ISLAND OF THE BLUE DOLPHINS."

From *Read It Again! More Book 2* published by GoodYearBooks. Copyright © 1991 Liz Rothlein and Terri Christman.

Name _____ Date _____

**ACTIVITY
SHEET 1**

Directions

Pretend that you are a TV reporter and that Karana has just arrived in your town after being found on the island on which she has survived alone for 18 years. You have been selected to report this as the headline news on your local TV station tonight at 6 p.m. In the space provided below, write the story you would present.

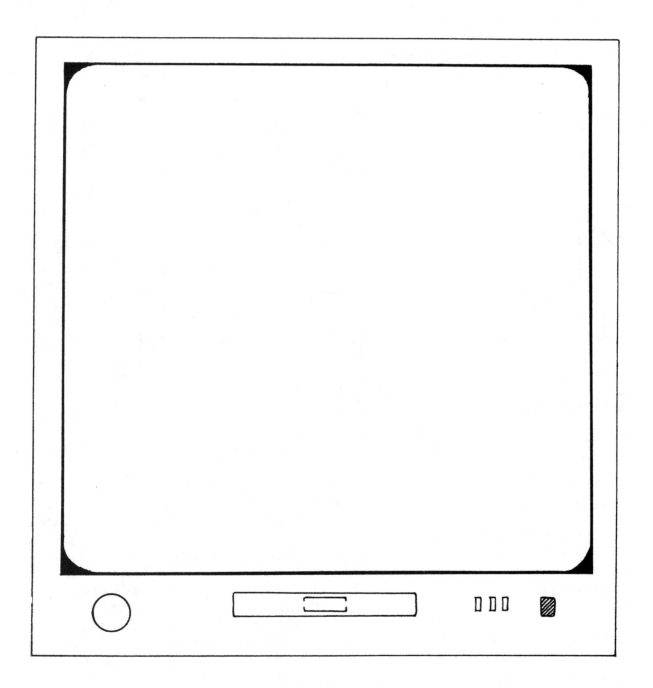

ISLAND OF THE BLUE DOLPHINS

ACTIVITY SHEET 2

Name _____ Date _____

Directions

Using the words in the box, complete the crossword puzzle below.

dune	dolphin	Ghalas-at	smelt	pitch	Ulape	mesa	Ramo	Tutok
Klimki	otters	Rontu	reef	cove	kelp	cliff	island	starfish
devilfish	Aleuts	crevice	gorge	abalones	ravine	league		

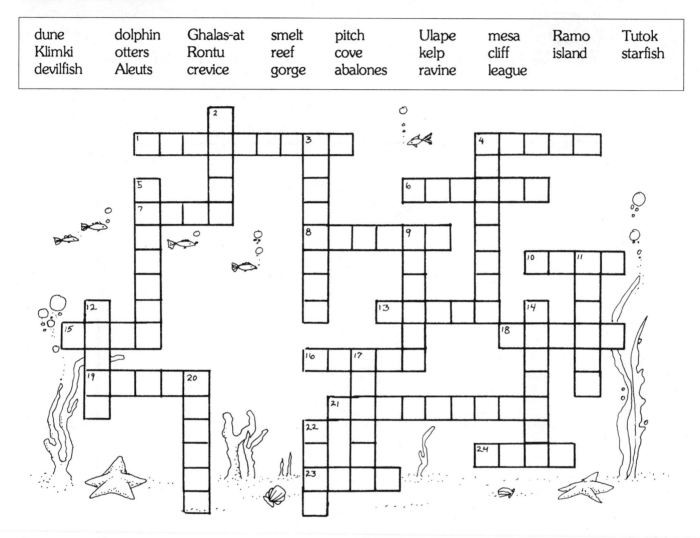

Across

1. Karana's village
4. Lighted the darkness when burned
6. Where Karana lived
7. Ridge of rock near the water's edge
8. What the Aleuts hunted
10. Seaweed
13. Black, tarlike substance
15. Small, protected bay
16. Karana's sister
18. Narrow canyon with steep, rocky walls
19. Aleut girlfriend
21. Fish with many arms (octopus)
23. High, flat plateau of land
24. Hill of sand built up by the wind

Down

2. Steep, rocky slope along a coastline
3. Basic shell food of the island
4. Sea animal with five arms that clung to the abalone
5. Small crack in a rocky hillside
9. Pathway between two hillsides
11. Approximately 3 miles in distance
12. Leader of wild dogs that became a pet
14. Fish for which the island was named
17. Hunters from the north
20. Chief who replaced Karana's father
22. Karana's brother

Name _____ Date _____

**ACTIVITY
SHEET 3**

Directions
The following are all adjectives that describe Karana's character. For each adjective, describe one incident from the story that best reveals that trait.

1. resourceful _____

_____

2. shy _____

_____

3. loyal _____

_____

4. sensitive _____

_____

5. stubborn _____

_____

6. caring _____

_____

7. foolish _____

_____

8. fearful _____

_____

9. aggressive _____

_____

10. brave _____

_____

Of all these traits, which do you feel is the most important for you to have or acquire?
_____ Why? _____

_____

ISLAND OF THE BLUE DOLPHINS

Additional Activities

1 Remind students that in this story Karana had to be prepared to leave her home quickly and that she could take with her only what she could carry in three baskets. Allow students 10 minutes to list what they would take from their homes if they could take only what would fit into three baskets. After they make their lists, ask them to prioritize the items, with number 1 being most important. Allow time for students to share their lists with one another.

2 This story focuses on Karana, a girl who lived alone on San Nicolas, one of the eight Channel Islands, which are about 75 miles southwest of Los Angeles. This island was visited by the Aleuts, who came to hunt otters. Using a world map, help students locate the Aleutian Islands off the coast of Alaska and San Nicolas off the coast of California. Finally, trace the path of the Aleuts from their islands to San Nicolas. Project how long it may have taken them to make the trip.

3 Divide the class into two groups, and assign each group one of the following research topics: (a) the Aleuts or (b) the eight Channel Islands off the southwest coast of California. Allow time for students to share their findings.

4 *Island of the Blue Dolphins* is a story about a courageous young girl. Ask students to think of other books they have read that portray a character with courage and strength, such as *Call It Courage* by Armstrong Sperry; *Julie of the Wolves* by Jean Craighead George; and *Robinson Crusoe* by Daniel Defoe. Provide each student with a 5 × 8 inch index card, and ask them to provide a book title, the author, and a brief paragraph describing a story they would recommend that demonstrates courage. Remind students that they may want to recommend biographies. Prepare a card file that is available to all students.

From *Read It Again! More Book 2* published by GoodYearBooks. Copyright © 1991 Liz Rothlein and Terri Christman.

TUCK EVER-LASTING

Author
Natalie Babbitt

Publisher
Farrar, Straus & Giroux, 1975

Pages 139	Reading Level Gr. 5	Interest Level Gr. 4–7

Other Books by Babbitt
The Devil's Storybook; Eyes of the Amaryllis; Goody Hall; Herbert Rowbarge; Kneeknock Rise; Phoebe's Revolt; The Search for Delicious; The Something; The Devil's Other Storybook; Duck Foote and the Sharks; Nellie, a Cat On Her Own

Information About the Author
Natalie Babbitt was born in Dayton, Ohio, on June 28, 1932. She married Samuel Fisher Babbitt, who is now vice president for development of Brown University in Providence, Rhode Island. They have three children and two grandchildren.

While in college, Natalie Babbitt majored in art; she entered the children's book field as an illustrator. She then became the author of many award-winning books for children. In 1969 *The Search for Delicious* was cited by the *New York Times* as the best book for children ages nine to twelve. *Kneeknock* and *The Devil's Storybook* were awarded American Library Association Notable Book Awards. *Kneeknock* was also awarded the Newbery Honor Book Award. *Goody Hall* was the Book World Spring Festival honor book.

Summary
The Tuck family is blessed—or cursed—with eternal life after they drink water from the magic spring in the woods. Winnie Foster, a ten-year-old girl, stumbles upon their secret. The Tucks take Winnie home with them so they can try to explain to her that living forever is not such a blessing as it may seem. The whole situation becomes more complicated when a stranger in a yellow suit follows them, discovers their secret, and decides to sell the spring water to make a fortune. For the sake of humankind, Winnie and the Tucks stop him so they can keep the secret.

Introduction
The Tuck family drank from a freshwater spring in a woods on the edge of the town of Treegap. From that day on, none of the Tucks grew any older. They became immortal. How do you think you would feel if you just found out you were going to live forever? Who would you tell? What would you do?

Vocabulary Words
roust	tangent	oppressive	consolingly
perversely	grimace	infinite	illiterates
revulsion	petulance	elation	accomplice
contemplation	constable	self-deprecation	

Discussion Questions

1 Do you think *Tuck Everlasting* is a good title for this book? Why or why not? (answers may vary)

2 What do you think would have happened if Mae hadn't killed the man in the yellow suit? (answers may vary)

3 Do you think it was a good or bad decision for Winnie to pour the magic water on the toad? Explain. (answers may vary)

4 What did the Tuck family do to keep other people from noticing that the Tucks were not getting older? (answers may vary but might include they kept moving and kept to themselves)

5 If you could have a drink of the springwater that the Tucks drank and knew you would live forever, at what age would you choose to drink it? Why? (answers may vary)

6 Mae Tuck felt that living forever was more of a curse than a blessing. Why do you think she felt this way? (answers may vary)

7 Compare and contrast the lifestyle of the Tuck family with the lifestyle of the Foster family. Which do you think Winnie preferred? Explain. (answers may vary)

8 What did you find out about Winnie from the inscription on her tombstone? (answers may vary but might include she never drank the springwater, she lived to be seventy-eight years old, and she was a wife and a mother)

Bulletin Board
Put the following caption on the bulletin board: "IF I COULD LIVE FOREVER, I WOULD . . ." Then provide students with 5 × 8 inch file cards and tell them to copy the caption onto the card and complete it. Fasten the completed cards to the bulletin board, and provide time for students to read the others' cards.

From *Read It Again! More Book 2* published by GoodYearBooks. Copyright © 1991 Liz Rothlein and Terri Christman.

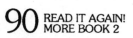

TUCK
EVERLASTING

Name _____ Date _____

Directions

The man in the yellow suit planned to sell the water from the spring. He said, "I'm not going to sell it to just anybody—only to certain people, people who deserve it." He also said it would be very expensive. Pretend you are the man in the yellow suit and that you own the spring with the magic water.

First, determine the criteria for deciding who would be eligible to buy the water:

1. _____

2. _____

3. _____

4. _____

5. _____

Second, in the space provided, create a poster or sign advertising the water. Include things like cost, who is eligible, how to get it, where to come, what it will do, and guarantees.

TUCK EVERLASTING

Name _____ Date _____

Directions

Using the continuums below, rate each of the characters identified in the box. To best indicate your perceptions of each character, put the symbol found in parentheses following each name somewhere between the two ends of the continuum.

Mae Tuck (X)	man in the yellow suit (O)	yourself (+)	Winnie (I)	Jessie (/)	Pa Tuck (^)

friendly _____ unfriendly

kind _____ cruel

happy _____ sad

brave _____ cowardly

wise _____ foolish

honest _____ dishonest

content _____ discontent

mature _____ immature

outgoing _____ shy

neat _____ untidy

unselfish _____ selfish

humorous _____ serious

Which of these characters (including yourself) do you believe possesses the most positive traits? _____

Explain. _____

_____

Using the back of this page, create your own continuums by selecting other qualities that you feel are important, such as popular–unpopular, ambitious–lazy, sociable–unsociable. Use these continuums to rate friends, relatives, and other book characters.

From *Read It Again! More Book 2* published by GoodYearBooks. Copyright © 1991 Liz Rothlein and Terri Christman.

Name _____ Date _____

Directions
Complete the following:

1. In many ways, the Tucks did not appreciate being immortal and destined to live forever. Yet most people you know would consider living forever the biggest blessing they could ever expect. In the spaces provided, list the advantages and disadvantages if indeed everyone could live forever.

Advantages

_____

_____

_____

Disadvantages

_____

_____

_____

2. Now pretend that everyone in the world could drink the water the Tucks drank and could choose to live forever. How would the world be different? Write a short story about a world without death. Use the back of this page if necessary.

_____

_____

_____

_____

_____

_____

_____

TUCK EVERLASTING

Additional Activities

1 In the story *Tuck Everlasting,* Jesse is only 17 years old. However, he has been like a 17-year-old for 87 years and therefore alive for 104 years. Tell students to pretend that, whatever their age is, they have been that age for 87 years. Next ask them to calculate the year they would have been born. For example, a student who is 11 years old in 1991, adding the 87 years already lived, would have been born in 1893. Then ask students to find and list at least ten major historical events that have taken place since their "pretend birth dates." Provide time for students to share their choices.

2 Winnie Foster's real name is Winifred Foster. Point out that people with names like James, Robert, Jennifer, and Elizabeth are often called by nicknames—Jim, Bob, Jenny, and Liz. Discuss with students why they think this happens. How did nicknames originate? What are the advantages and disadvantages of nicknames? Finally, allow time for students to share their nicknames and to tell how they got them and how they feel about them. Ask students who do not have nicknames to think of nicknames for themselves.

3 Ask each student to select one of the characters from *Tuck Everlasting* and then create a list of questions to ask that character. These questions can investigate the characters' feelings, attitudes, actions, and so forth. For example, if Jesse were to be interviewed, he might be asked, "How did you feel about leaving Winnie?" "Did you think Winnie would drink the magic water when she was seventeen years old and come to find you?" "What were your plans for you and Winnie if she drank the magic water when she was seventeen and found you?" Once the questions have been formulated, let a student become the character that he or she wrote questions for and another student become the interviewer.

4 Tell each student to select a specific event that happened in *Tuck Everlasting.* Provide each student with an 8½ × 11 inch piece of construction paper. Tell students to summarize their events in writing and to illustrate them on the sheet of paper. Next, allow time for students to share their work and determine the correct sequence of events. Create a story time line with these events. If more than one student selects the same event, simply cluster their work on the time line.

5 Discuss with students the fact that, throughout history, people have searched for ways to live forever. For example, Spanish explorer Juan Ponce de Léon claimed to have found the fountain of youth in St. Augustine, Florida. Ask students to investigate other historical attempts to live forever by asking friends, neighbors, and relatives. Allow them a week to gather information. Finally, let them share the findings.

From *Read It Again! More Book 2* published by GoodYearBooks. Copyright © 1991 Liz Rothlein and Terri Christman.

TUCK
EVERLASTING

6 In the story *Tuck Everlasting*, each of the Tucks has a different attitude toward or philosophy about being immortal. Write the following statements, which were taken from the book, on the chalkboard. Then divide students into four groups, assigning each group one of the statements to explain and defend.

MILES TUCK: "The way I see it, it's no good hiding yourself away like Pa and lots of other people. And it's no good just thinking of your own pleasure, either. People got to do something useful if they're going to take up space in the world."

JESSE TUCK: "Why, heck, Winnie, life's to enjoy yourself, isn't it? What else is it good for? That's what I say."

PA TUCK: "You can't have living without dying. So you can't call it living, what we got. We just *are*, we just *be*, like rocks beside the roads."

MA TUCK: "Life's got to be lived, no matter how long or how short. You got to take what comes."

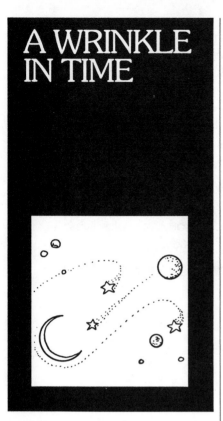

A WRINKLE IN TIME

Author
Madeleine L'Engle

Publisher
Dell, 1962

Pages	Reading Level	Interest Level
211	Gr. 5–8	Gr. 4–7

Other Books by L'Engle
The Arm of the Starfish; The Journey with Jonah; The Moon by Night; A Swiftly Tilting Planet; A Ring of Endless Light; A Wind in the Door

Information About the Author

Madeleine L'Engle was born on November 29, 1918 in New York City. She was an actress, a country storekeeper, a teacher, a lecturer, and a librarian. She began writing at the early age of five but wasn't encouraged to write by her family or her teachers. It was her actor husband who persuaded her to return to writing. Madeleine L'Engle won the John Newbery Medal for *A Wrinkle in Time* in 1963; this book also received the Sequoyah Award in 1965, the Lewis Carrol Shelf Award in 1965, and the Hans Christian Andersen Award in 1968. *The Moon by Night* received the Austrian State Literature Award in 1969. In 1980 *A Swiftly Tilting Planet* won the American Book Award, and in 1981 she authored *A Ring of Endless Light*, which won the John Newbery Honor Book Award. With all this success, however, Madeleine L'Engle has had her share of rejection slips. In fact, *A Wrinkle in Time* was rejected by a publisher.

Madeleine L'Engle has written books and plays most of her life. She has traveled extensively throughout the United States and Europe.

Summary

Meg, her younger brother Charles Wallace, and her friend Calvin go on a mysterious adventure in search of Meg and Charles Wallace's father. With the help of Mrs. Whatsit, Mrs. Who, and Mrs. Which, plus other extraterrestrial creatures, the children overcome all the hurdles they encounter.

Introduction

The title of this book is *A Wrinkle in Time*. What do you think it means? What do you think the book will be about?

Vocabulary Words

ineffable	incomprehensible	vicious	prodigious
dubiously	sullen	ephemeral	inadvertently
annihilate	pedantic	tenacity	propitious
diverting	reverberated	anguished	precipitously

From *Read It Again! More Book 2* published by GoodYearBooks. Copyright © 1991 Liz Rothlein and Terri Christman.

A WRINKLE IN TIME

Discussion Questions

1 Explain in your own words what a tesseract is. (answers may vary)

2 Meg, Calvin, and Charles Wallace did not have a lot of trouble accepting all the different beings they encountered, such as Mrs. Whatsit, Mrs. Who, Mrs. Which, the beasts in Ixchel, and the creatures of Uriel. How do you think you would have reacted? (answers may vary)

3 What do you think the Black Thing was? (answers may vary)

4 Why do you think Mr. Murray was imprisoned? (answers may vary)

5 Why do you think Charles Wallace acted the way he did when he got to Camazotz? (answers may vary)

6 How did Meg react when she found out that Charles Wallace had been left in Camazotz? Why do you think she acted in this manner? (answers may vary)

7 What is something in this story that could really have happened? (answers my vary)

8 What is something in this story that could not really happen? (answers may vary)

Bulletin Board

Put the caption "WHO AM I?" on the bulletin board. Point out that there are no illustrations in *A Wrinkle in Time*. Ask students to select one of the characters from the book to depict, and provide each with a 9 × 12 inch sheet of paper. Have them write "Who Am I?" across the bottom of the sheet, illustrate the character they have selected, and fasten the paper to the bulletin board. Allow time for students to make guesses about others' illustrations. Finally, group the illustrations of each character together and compare and contrast them.

Name _____ Date _____

Directions
Meg encountered the following planets on her journey to find her missing father: Uriel, Ixchel, and Camazotz. Look at the illustrations below, and then identify each of the planets.

1. Name of Planet _____

2. Name of Planet _____

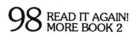

3. Name of Planet _____

If you had to select one of these three planets to live on, which would you select?

_____

Why? _____

_____

_____

_____

_____

_____

Name _____ Date _____

Directions

Pretend that now you would like to read more about the Murrays. For example, you may want to know whether Meg, Charles Wallace, and Calvin continue traveling with Mrs. Whatsit. Or if Charles Wallace would behave differently. Or what Mr. Murray will do once he is back on Earth. Write a letter to Madeline L'Engle, suggesting that she write a sequel. You might suggest a title for the new book, the things you'd like to have included, any new characters that might be added, at what point in the Murrays' life you'd like to see the book end, or some other idea. Finally, share your ideas with your classmates, and then mail the letters to the publisher of *A Wrinkle in Time* for forwarding to Madeleine L'Engle.

ACTIVITY SHEET 2

_____ (Date)

Dear Ms. L'Engle:

Sincerely,

Name _____ Date _____

**ACTIVITY
SHEET 3**

Directions
The phrases and sentences below can be found in the book.
Look at the underlined words. Find at least two other words that
mean the same as each underlined word, and write them in the
spaces provided. Finally, put a check to the left of the word that
you think would be the best substitute for the word in the phrase.

1. There was an air of <u>ineffable</u> peace . . . .

_____ _____ _____

2. "Yah," Meg said <u>dubiously</u>.

_____ _____ _____

3. "Surely her mother must know what people were saying, she must be aware of the
smugly <u>vicious</u> gossip."

_____ _____ _____

4. Charles said, "Impressive, isn't it?" "<u>Prodigious</u>," Mrs. Murray said.

_____ _____ _____

5. When Mrs. Whatsit sighed it seemed completely <u>incomprehensible</u>.

_____ _____ _____

6. . . . she gets <u>sullen</u> and stubborn and sets up a fine mental block for herself.

_____ _____ _____

7. . . . Meg felt that Mrs. Which, despite her looks and <u>ephemeral</u> broomstick, was
someone in whom one could put complete trust.

_____ _____ _____

8. "You tell me, you see, sort of <u>inadvertently</u>."

_____ _____ _____

9. "It is so much kinder simply to <u>annihilate</u> anyone who is ill."

_____ _____ _____

10. His voice took on the dry, <u>pedantic</u> tones of Mr. Jenkins.

_____ _____ _____

Additional Activities

1 Ask students to read other books by Madeleine L'Engle such as *The Moon by Night*, *A Swiftly Tilting Planet*, or *A Ring of Endless Light*. Have them compare and contrast these books with one another, as well as with *A Wrinkle in Time*.

2 *A Wrinkle in Time* includes many aphorisms or proverbs. For example:

"Faith is the sister of justice."
"Nothing deters a good man from doing what is honorable."
"The road to hell is paved with good intentions."

Explain to students that an aphorism is a brief statement of principle similar to a proverb, which is a short saying that expresses a well-known fact or truth. Tell students to ask their parents or grandparents for other aphorisms or proverbs or to research to find one. Then tell them to write their aphorism or proverb on a 9 × 12 inch sheet of paper, to write in their own words what it means, and then to illustrate it. Finally, put these papers together into a class book of aphorisms and proverbs.

3 Ask students to choose their favorite character from *A Wrinkle in Time*. Give each a 9 × 12 inch sheet of paper for writing the name of the character, illustrating the character, and telling why he or she selected that character. Finally, group students who chose the same character so they can discuss their reasons for liking that character.

4 The word "tesseract" was used in this story to mean a wrinkle in time. Using the letters in "tesseract," create a class acrostic; each letter of *A Wrinkle in Time*. The first one is done for you.

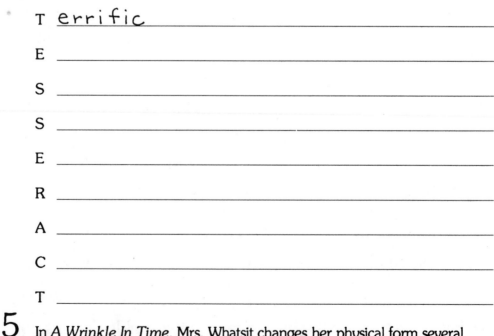

T errific

E _____

S _____

S _____

E _____

R _____

A _____

C _____

T _____

5 In *A Wrinkle In Time*, Mrs. Whatsit changes her physical form several times. Ask students to think about how they would change their bodies if they had that kind of power. Provide time for students to share their ideas.

A WRINKLE IN TIME

6 There are nine known major planets in the solar system: Mercury, Venus, Earth, Mars, Jupiter, Saturn, Uranus, Neptune, and Pluto. Divide the class into eight groups, and assign each group a planet to research (exclude Earth). Once the research is completed, ask students to recall the planets described in *A Wrinkle in Time*. Are there any similarities between the fictitious planets and the real planets? If so, describe what they are. If not, where do students think the author got her ideas for the planets created in the book?

7 Some students may be interested in reading more about life in outer space. Provide them with the names of the following authors who have written on this subject: Carl Sagan, Isaac Asimov, Ursula LeGuin, Arthur Clarke.

8 In our society, Mr. Murray would be considered a missing person. Call the local police station and ask someone to come to your class to discuss the procedures for reporting a person who is missing. Ask the person who is visiting to show the students a Missing Persons Report form. If possible, duplicate this form and ask students to fill it out, reporting Mr. Murray as a missing person.

APPENDIX

GENERAL ACTIVITY 1

Directions

Do the crossword puzzle by completing the sentences.

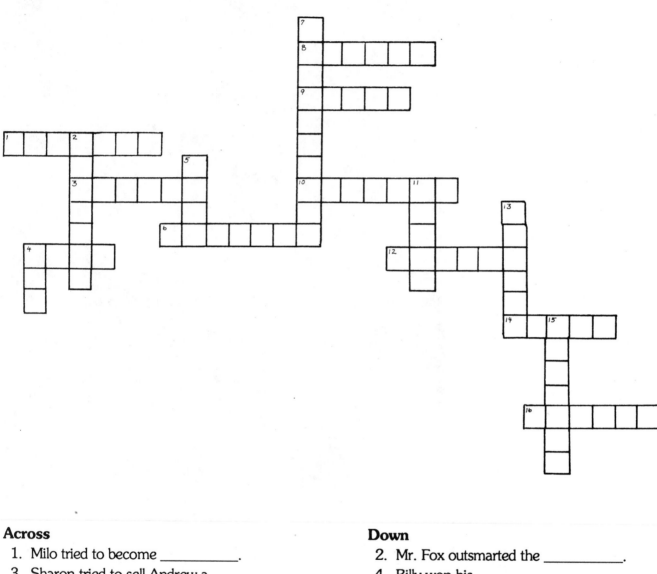

Across

1. Milo tried to become _____.
3. Sharon tried to sell Andrew a _____.
4. Margalo was Stuart Little's _____.
6. Meg's adventure took her to different _____.
8. Karana lived on an _____.
9. Leigh Botts kept a _____.
10. Tuck had _____ life.
12. Winnie learned about the Tucks' _____.
14. The third graders _____ Partner.
16. The Borrowers were very _____.

Down

2. Mr. Fox outsmarted the _____.
4. Billy won his _____.
5. The Velveteen Rabbit became _____.
7. Sarah traveled through the _____.
11. Pippi's mother was an _____.
13. The Aleuts hunted _____.
15. Chester thought Bunnicula was a _____ bunny.

From *Read It Again! More Book 2* published by GoodYearBooks. Copyright © 1991 Liz Rothlein and Terri Christman.

Name _____ Date _____

GENERAL ACTIVITY 2

Directions
Below is a list of some of the main characters and titles of the books you have read. Mark the face to express how you feel about each character.

1. Milo (*Be a Perfect Person in Just Three Days*)

2. Sarah (*The Courage of Sarah Noble*)

3. Andrew (*Freckle Juice*)

4. Leigh (*Dear Mr. Henshaw*)

5. Billy (*How to Eat Fried Worms*)

6. Stuart (*Stuart Little*)

7. Meg (*A Wrinkle in Time*)

8. Pippi (*Pippi Longstocking*)

9. Karana (*Island of the Blue Dolphins*)

10. Tuck (*Tuck Everlasting*)

11. Harold (*Bunnicula*)

12. Brad (*Rent a Third Grader*)

Which character is your favorite? _____

Explain. _____

Which character is your least favorite? _____

Explain. _____

Which character is most like you? _____

Explain. _____

Name _____ Date _____

Directions

Below are the names of books; in the box are the names of characters from the books. Match each character with the correct book by putting the letter for the character in the blank.

---

a. Dr. K. Pinkerton Silverfish   d. Alan   g. Charles Wallace
b. Andrew   e. Margalo   h. Ramo
c. Bandit   f. Bunce   i. Winnie

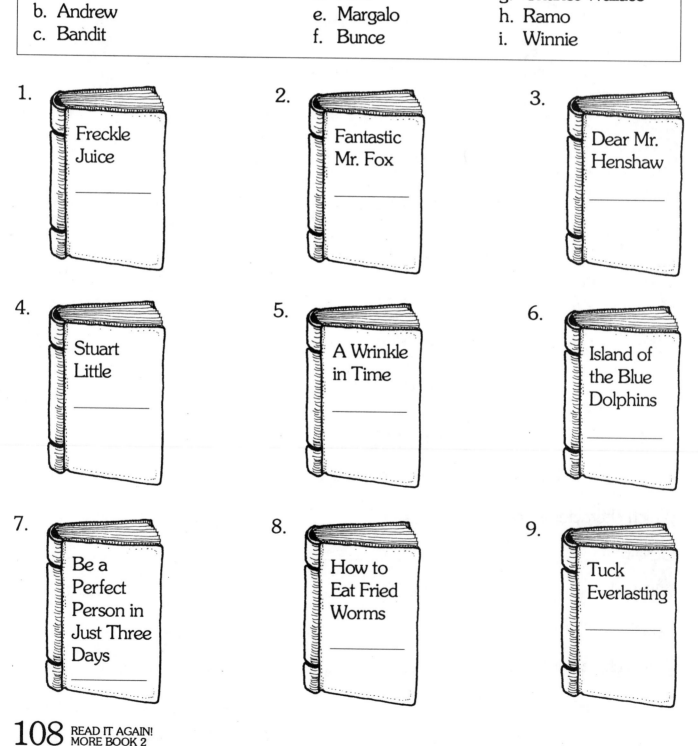

1. Freckle Juice _____

2. Fantastic Mr. Fox _____

3. Dear Mr. Henshaw _____

4. Stuart Little _____

5. A Wrinkle in Time _____

6. Island of the Blue Dolphins _____

7. Be a Perfect Person in Just Three Days _____

8. How to Eat Fried Worms _____

9. Tuck Everlasting _____

Name _____ Date _____

Directions

Select the character, from one of the fifteen books listed below, that you enjoyed the most or feel you know the best. Use the form that follows to create a bio-poem about the character you have chosen.

GENERAL ACTIVITY 4

Be a Perfect Person in Just Three Days
The Courage of Sarah Noble
The Velveteen Rabbit
How to Eat Fried Worms
Rent a Third Grader

The Borrowers
Island of the Blue Dolphins
A Wrinkle in Time
Bunnicula
Freckle Juice

Dear Mr. Henshaw
Pippi Longstocking
Stuart Little
Fantastic Mr. Fox
Tuck Everlasting

Line 1: (first name) _____

Line 2: (title) _____

Line 3: (four words that describe the person) _____ ,

_____ , _____ , and _____

Line 4: Lover of (three or more things or ideas) _____ ,

_____ , and _____

Line 5: Who believed (one or more ideas) _____

Line 6: Who wanted (three things) _____ ,

_____ , and _____

Line 7: Who used (three things or methods) _____ ,

_____ , and _____

Line 8: Who gave (three things) _____ ,

_____ , and _____

Line 9: Who said (a quote) " _____

_____ . "

Line 10: (last name) _____

From *Read It Again! More Book 2* published by GoodYearBooks. Copyright © 1991 Liz Rothlein and Terri Christman.

GENERAL ACTIVITY 5

Directions
After you have read *Island of the Blue Dolphins, The Courage of Sarah Noble, A Wrinkle in Time,* and *Tuck Everlasting,* illustrate their settings in the boxes.

Island of the Blue Dolphins	*The Courage of Sarah Noble*
A Wrinkle in Time	*Tuck Everlasting*

How are these settings similar? _____

_____

How are these settings different? _____

_____

Which setting did you like best? _____

Why? _____

_____

From *Read It Again! More Book 2* published by GoodYearBooks. Copyright © 1991 Liz Rothlein and Terri Christman.

Directions

Read the book titles below and select five that you would like to change. Create a new title for each book, and then tell why you chose that title.

GENERAL
ACTIVITY 6

*Be a Perfect Person in Just
    Three Days*
The Courage of Sarah Noble
The Velveteen Rabbit
How to Eat Fried Worms
Rent a Third Grader

The Borrowers
*Island of the Blue
    Dolphins*
A Wrinkle in Time
Bunnicula
Freckle Juice

Dear Mr. Henshaw
Pippi Longstocking
Stuart Little
Fantastic Mr. Fox
Tuck Everlasting

1. I would change the title of _____

    to _____ ,

    because _____ .

2. I would change the title of _____

    to _____ ,

    because _____ .

3. I would change the title of _____

    to _____ ,

    because _____ .

4. I would change the title of _____

    to _____ ,

    because _____ .

5. I would change the title of _____

    to _____ ,

    because _____ .

Directions

Select an author that you would like to know more about. If the author is still living, write him or her a letter asking for specific information. If this is not possible, visit the library and consult *Something About the Author: Facts and Pictures About Authors and Illustrators of Books for Young Children*, which is an ongoing reference series. Authors' addresses can often be found in this book, or letters can be sent to the author via the publisher. Another reference source is *Yesterday's Authors for Children*, a two-volume set focusing on early authors and illustrators (from the beginnings of children's literature through 1960) whose books are being read by children today.

Once you have obtained information about the author, complete the following:

GENERAL ACTIVITY 7

1. Name of author: _____

Is this the author's real name or a pseudonym (a name that is made up)? _____

If the name used is a pseudonym, what is the author's real name? _____

_____

2. How many books has the author written for children? _____

3. What is your favorite book that this author has written? _____

4. Why does the author write books for children? _____

_____

5. Where does the author get his or her ideas for writing books? _____

_____

6. What career(s), if any, has the author had besides writing? _____

_____

7. What additional information did you find out about the author you researched?

_____

_____

From *Read It Again! More Book 2* published by GoodYearBooks. Copyright © 1991 Liz Rothlein and Terri Christman.

Directions

A fact is something that can be proven as true. For example, "Airplanes can fly" is a fact. An opinion is something that cannot be proven as true. For example, "Flying is fun" is an opinion. Read the following statements. Put an *F* in the blank if the statement is a fact. Put an *O* in the blank if the statement is an opinion.

GENERAL ACTIVITY 8

_____ 1. The Velveteen Rabbit was a stuffed toy.

_____ 2. Milo wore broccoli around his neck because it was the most nutritious vegetable available.

_____ 3. Andrew Marcus wanted freckles just like Nicky Lane.

_____ 4. The Velveteen Rabbit liked being with the boy.

_____ 5. Leigh Botts was a good letter writer.

_____ 6. Mrs. Whatsit, Mrs. Who, and Mrs. Which were extraterrestrial creatures.

_____ 7. Billy was stupid for making a bet to eat fifteen worms.

_____ 8. Sarah traveled through the wilderness.

_____ 9. Karana knew how to provide for herself.

_____ 10. Leigh Botts had more problems than most children his age.

_____ 11. Billy ate fifteen worms.

_____ 12. Sarah Noble liked living in the wilderness.

_____ 13. Pippi lived with a monkey.

_____ 14. The Tucks were glad they could live forever.

_____ 15. The police department was going to sell Partner to the HappiPet Food Company.

_____ 16. Bunnicula was a vampire bunny.

_____ 17. Pippi's next-door neighbors were Tommy and Annika.

_____ 18. *The Borrowers* was written by Mary Norton.

_____ 19. Harold ate chocolate cupcakes with cream filling.

_____ 20. It rained the day Brad had his car wash.

From *Read It Again! More Book 2* published by GoodYearBooks. Copyright © 1991 Liz Rothlein and Terri Christman.

Name _____ Date _____

Directions

Specific literary elements (characterization, plot, theme, setting, point of view) are used to develop a story. The way these elements are developed makes the difference between a good piece of literature and a bad piece of literature. The following explanations of literary elements can help you evaluate the books you read.

Characterization: Developing and revealing characters through conversation, actions, and behaviors; through narrations; and through comments of others
Plot: The story line, the happenings that keep the reader involved and interested in the book
Theme: The message or feeling that the author is trying to convey
Setting: The where and when, which transport the reader to the time and place of the story
Point of view: The person through whose eyes the story unfolds—first person (I) or third person (he/she/they)

Using the following scale, grade each literary element of a book you have read. Comment on why you assigned the grades you did.

Grading Scale:
A = excellent
B = good
C = fair
D = not very good
F = not good

Title of Book _____

Author _____

Grade	Literary Element	Comments
_____	Characterization	_____
_____	Plot	_____
_____	Theme	_____
_____	Setting	_____
_____	Point of view	_____

From *Read It Again! More Book 2* published by GoodYearBooks. Copyright © 1991 Liz Rothlein and Terri Christman.

From *Read It Again! More Book 2* published by GoodYearBooks. Copyright © 1991 Liz Rothlein and Terri Christman.

Name _____ Date _____

Directions

In libraries, books are categorized by genres, which have certain characteristics. Some common genres are picture books, realistic fiction, historical fiction, fantasy, folktales, poetry, informational books, and biographies. Often it is easy to figure out which genre a book belongs to, yet many books overlap genres. (For more detailed information on genres, refer to *The Literature Connection* by Liz Rothlein and Anita Meinbach, *Children and Books* by Zena Sutherland and May Hill Arbuthnot, and *Children's Literature in the Elementary School* by Charlotte S. Huck, Susan Hepler, and Janet Hickman.) Using the brief descriptions of genres provided below, categorize each of the books you have read.

GENERAL ACTIVITY 10

Genre Descriptions

Realistic fiction: Fictitious but set in a plausible time and place. Realistic fiction often focuses on everyday problems, such as family issues, interpersonal problems, handicaps, sexism, aging, and death.

Historical fiction: Realistic and set in the past. One type of historical fiction is written about the past but uses fictional characters; there are no real people or recorded events, and yet the reader gets a feeling for the period about which the book was written. Another type of historical fiction involves actual people and recorded events.

Fantasy: Stories of enchantment, humorous tales, stories in which animals and toys are personified, and tales of science fiction. Fantasy books blend things that really couldn't happen in real life with realistic detail. Good fantasy involves at least one element of the possible within a framework of reality.

Books to Classify by Genre

Be a Perfect Person in Just Three Days   *Bunnicula*
The Courage of Sarah Noble   *Freckle Juice*
The Velveteen Rabbit   *Dear Mr. Henshaw*
How to Eat Fried Worms   *Pippi Longstocking*
Rent a Third Grader   *Stuart Little*
The Borrowers   *Fantastic Mr. Fox*
Island of the Blue Dolphins   *Tuck Everlasting*
A Wrinkle in Time

Realistic Fiction

Historical Fiction

Fantasy

Name _____ Date _____

Directions

Using a large sheet of paper (18 × 24 inches), make a poster about one of your favorite books. Be creative so it will capture attention and make others want to read the book. Be sure to include the names of the book and the author. You might also include an illustration. Display the poster when it is completed. *Note:* Plan your poster by making a sketch of it in the space provided.

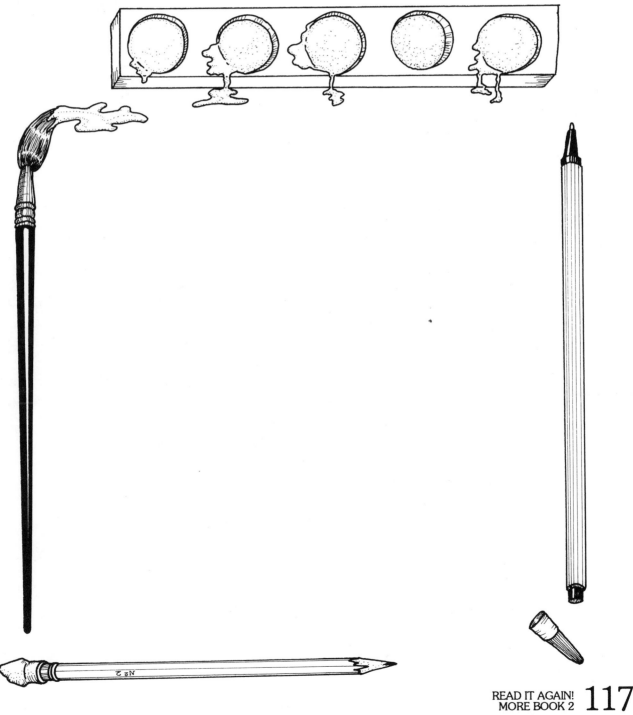

Directions
Write a telegram, in twenty-five words or less, describing a
favorite character in a book you've read.

WESTERN UNION

_____

_____

_____

_____

_____

_____

_____

_____

_____

_____

_____

_____

Name _____ Date _____

BOOK REPORT 3

Directions
Make a report of a book you have read by filling in the blanks.

Title of book: _____

_____

Author: _____

_____

Illustrator: _____

_____

Publisher: _____

_____

Copyright date: _____

Illustrate and write about the character
you would most like to have as a friend.
Explain your choice.

Illustrate and write about your favorite
part of the book.

After completing the inside of the book, cut it out and fold on the dotted line. Then draw
a new cover for the book.

Name _____ Date _____

Directions

Book reviews are published in a variety of journals and magazines to help other people decide whether they would like to read the book. Write a book review of your favorite book, and compile it with other reviews written by your classmates. Include the following:

1. Biographical information: author, title, publisher, and publication date
2. Brief summary of the story
3. Description of the main character(s)
4. Problem or conflict described in the story
5. Clue as to how the problem was solved
6. Your opinion of the book and your reason for that opinion

Also include a creative headline, an illustration, and a caption to go with the illustration.

Headline _____

Review _____

_____

_____

_____

_____

_____

Illustration   Caption _____

_____

_____

_____

_____

VOCABULARY WORDS

The following words are introduced and reinforced throughout this book.

accomplice
admonition
agony
aimed
alert
ancestors
anguished
annihilate
antidote
apoplectically
astonishment
astounded

belittling
blur
bracken
burrows

camouflaged
canape
cannibal
carcass
cavorting
chaff
chaos
chattering
chortle
clambered
clockwork
commands
commonplace
consolingly
constable
consumption
contemplation
contented
contradicted
cooperated
cormorants
courageous
crept
cross-country
crouched

deliberate
deny

desperate
digress
discernible
disdainfully
disinfected
dismayed
diverting
drenching
drifted
dubiously
dusk
dwarf

elation
enormous
ephemeral
essential
exhausted
expedition

faggot
fantastic
farmer
feast
fictitious
firming
fledglings
foliage
foreigner
formula
fortress
fraught
fronds
fungus

gazing
generation
glowered
gondola
gore
gorge
grimace
guaranteed

halyard
handsome

hauncher
heather
humiliating

illiterates
impatience
inadvertently
incomprehensible
indulgent
ineffable
infant
infinite
injustice
innocent
inquired
inspected

jeers
jostled

lair
loped

majestically
manage
masterminded
mechanical
menacingly
mimeographed
moccasins
modestly
molest
mortar

narrative
nuisance
nutritious

obsequiously
obstinate
omen
oppressive
outlandish
outsmarted
overwrought

palisade
partition
passage
patiently
pedantic
peered
perfection
persuade
perversely
pestle
petulance
playmate
precipitously
precisely
prey
prodigious
promenade
prominent
promptly
propitious
prowling

quivers

radiant
ravenous
ravine
reassuring
recipe
reeks
refinery
reflection
reminded
rent
reproachfully
repulsive
retain
reverberated
reverie
revulsion
ridiculous
rig
rivalry
roust

sauntering
savages
sawdust
scanned
self-deprecation
sensible
sensitive
shabbier
shrill
shy
sinews
smirking
smoldering
solemn
solemnly
sorrow
souvenir
squaw
stalking
stealthily
subtle
sullen

tangent
tenacity
tentatively
threshold
tilted
tranquil
trench
trundled
twitched

vaguely
vanquished
velveteen
ventilation
vicious
vigorous

wafted
wailing
wigwam
wondering

ANSWER KEY

Be a Perfect Person in Just Three Days

ACTIVITY SHEET 2

1. e
2. f
3. h
4. j
5. i
6. b
7. d
8. a
9. g
10. c

Bunnicula

ACTIVITY SHEET 1

Harold
  2. He was telling this story.
  4. He got to eat the steak.

Bunnicula
  1. He was sitting in a shoebox with a piece of paper tied with a ribbon around his neck.
  5. He drank carrot juice.

Chester
  3. He developed a taste for reading early in life.
  6. He tried to warn the family about the vampire bunny.

ACTIVITY SHEET 2

1. reality
2. fantasy
3. reality
4. fantasy
5. fantasy
6. reality
7. reality
8. reality
9. fantasy
10. reality

The Velveteen Rabbit

ACTIVITY SHEET 1

1. Skin Horse to Rabbits
2. Rabbits to Skin Horse
3. Nana to Boy
4. Boy to Nana
5. Fairy to Rabbits
6. Rabbits to Velveteen Rabbit
7. Rabbits to Velveteen Rabbit
8. Doctor to Nana
9. Fairy to Velveteen Rabbit
10. Skin Horse to Velveteen Rabbit

ACTIVITY SHEET 2

1. F
2. O
3. O
4. O
5. F
6. O
7. O
8. O
9. F
10. O
11. F
12. F
13. F
14. O
15. O

Dear Mr. Henshaw

ACTIVITY SHEET 2

1. desert
2. villains
3. controlling
4. their
5. principal
6. pinball
7. stomach
8. battery
9. burglar
10. thief

Rent a Third Grader

ACTIVITY SHEET 1

1. Louisa
2. Miss Bilgore
3. Partner
4. Brad
5. Jennie
6. Officer Chambliss

ACTIVITY SHEET 2

1. d
2. f
3. e
4. l
5. k
6. c
7. g
8. a
9. j
10. b
11. i
12. h

Stuart Little

ACTIVITY SHEET 1

1. pond, paper bag, referee, sailboat, wasp
2. Margalo, ocean, ice skates, scow, garbage
3. Harriet, river, canoe, birchbark, paddle
4. string, slimy, ring, drain, tub

ACTIVITY SHEET 2

1. Margalo
2. Mrs. Little
3. Stuart
4. Stuart
5. George
6. Stuart
7. Stuart
8. Margalo
9. pigeon
10. Dr. Paul Carey
11. superintendent
12. Stuart

From *Read It Again! More Book 2* published by GoodYearBooks. Copyright © 1991 Liz Rothlein and Terri Christman.

Fantastic Mr. Fox

ACTIVITY SHEET 1
1. Boggis   3. Bean   4. Bunce
2. Mr. Fox   4. Rat   5. Mr. Badger

ACTIVITY SHEET 2
Things That Could Happen
Foxes living in a hole
Farmers shooting a fox
The foxes eating chickens
Using a mechanical shovel to dig a hole
People laughing at the farmers
Mrs. Fox getting weak from lack of food and water

Things That Could Not Happen
The animals never going outside
Mr. Fox talking to his family
The animals having a feast at a table
The badger worrying about "stealing"
The farmers still waiting today for Mr. Fox
A rat sucking cider through a tube

Island of the Blue Dolphins

ACTIVITY SHEET 2

A Wrinkle in Time

ACTIVITY SHEET 1
1. Camazotz
2. Uriel
3. Ixchel

ACTIVITY SHEET 3
Answers may vary but might include the following:
1. indescribable, unspeakable
2. questionably, skeptically, doubtfully, uncertainly
3. cruel, evil, fierce, malevolent

4. fabulous, extravagant, marvelous, ominous, extraordinary
5. unknowable, unintelligible, unfathomable
6. dark, glum
7. short-lived, transitory
8. accidentally, unintentionally
9. butcher, massacre, slaughter, abolish
10. academic, bookish, scholastic

General Activities

GENERAL ACTIVITY 1

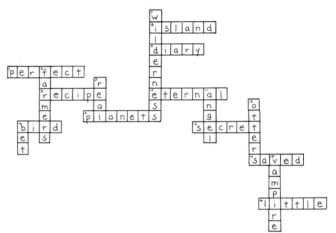

GENERAL ACTIVITY 3
1. *Freckle Juice*—b
2. *Fantastic Mr. Fox*—f
3. *Dear Mr. Henshaw*—c
4. *Stuart Little*—e
5. *A Wrinkle in Time*—g
6. *Island of the Blue Dolphins*—h
7. *Be a Perfect Person in Just Three Days*—a
8. *How to Eat Fried Worms*—d
9. *Tuck Everlasting*—i

GENERAL ACTIVITY 8
1. F	6. F	11. F	16. O
2. O	7. O	12. O	17. F
3. F	8. F	13. F	18. F
4. O	9. F	14. O	19. F
5. O	10. O	15. F	20. F

GENERAL ACTIVITY 10*
Realistic Fiction
Be a Perfect Person in Just Three Days
Freckle Juice
Dear Mr. Henshaw
How to Eat Fried Worms

*The books may fit into other genres as well.

Pippi Longstocking
Rent a Third Grader
Historical Fiction
The Courage of Sarah Noble
Island of the Blue Dolphins

Fantasy
Bunnicula
The Velveteen Rabbit
Stuart Little
The Borrowers
Fantastic Mr. Fox
Tuck Everlasting
A Wrinkle in Time

From *Read It Again! More Book 2* published by GoodYearBooks. Copyright © 1991 Liz Rothlein and Terri Christman.